FAKE AWAY

by Chef Adrian

FAKE AWAY

by Chef Adrian

FAST FOOD MADE HEALTHY

MERCIER PRESS

IRISH PUBLISHER – IRISH STORY

CONTENTS

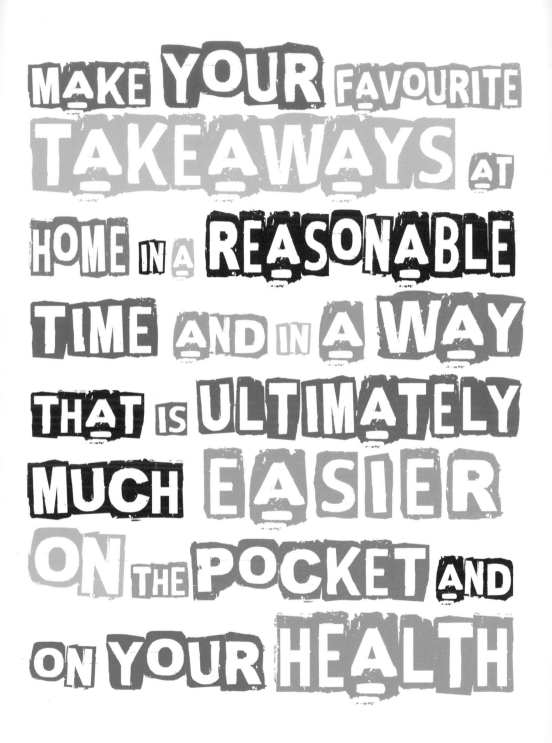

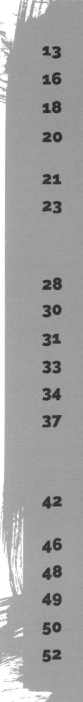

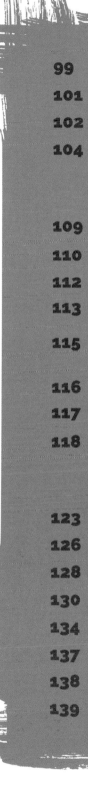

THAI

WESTERN EUROPE

SIDES

DESSERTS

ACKNOWLEDGEMENTS

First I'd like to thank you, the reader, for buying a copy of my book. You have made a young man's dream come true.

I would not have got to this point without the support and love of friends and family. To my dad, John, thanks for your great patience, and for the advice, help and time you have invested in me. Thanks to my mum, Anne, for putting up with all my messing, to my brothers and sister (Cathal, Baby Seán and Sarah), to Granny Susie, and to all my cousins, aunties and uncles. And finally, thanks to my two best friends for years – Damien Timmins and Brian McAveety (you are well bet).

Many organisations have supported me over the last few years and they all deserve a mention. First, a big thank you to the Associated Craft Butchers of Ireland, and all the butcher shops across the country that have supported me from the start. Mary, Carla and Tom Whelan from KAL/Nordmende in Citywest, you have been so kind and so helpful, and I will always be grateful. Martin Event Management provides me with fantastic support and I want to thank the company for the amount of work it puts into all my cookery demos and events across the country. Thank you also to Eoin O'Flynn and everyone in Flogas; Jack and everyone from Newgrange Gold; Fiontan Gogarty from Wildwood Vinegars; and all the Irish food producers who come to our shows. A special mention should go to the Cavan ones: Clare and Ciaran from Moran's Mega Jam; Alan Raymond and his son, Oisín, from Ciste Milis; Barry John and Aaron from

Barry Johns Sausages; and John Rowe from Mr Muffin. Finally a massive thank you to Marie O'Toole and everyone from the Irish Countrywomen's Association for your support.

A special mention should go to John Hickey – thank you.

I also cannot thank Hillary O'Callaghan and Alexandra Rooney from RTÉ enough for believing in me and for all their support and help. To Martin King, Lucy Kennedy and everyone involved in *The Six O'Clock Show* on TV3, I love working with you and long may it continue.

Marc Dillon and Robin Murray from NOMOS Ireland have helped me so much, as have Niall, Graham and all the gang at Lovin Dublin.

Last, but not least, a special mention must go to Fiona Coyne and all her family. Thank you for your support from the start, advice and for being amazing people.

INTRODUCTION

Writing this, it is hard for me to believe that, from starting off as a fourteen-year-old commis chef peeling spuds down the back of the kitchen, I now have my own cookbook. Fourteen may seem like a young age to start working in a kitchen and I am often asked why I started cooking so early in life. The answer is simple: school isn't for everyone and it definitely wasn't for me. I am in no way academic and never worried about studying, as I felt I'd never use any of the stuff I was supposed to be learning in the future. Instead I used school to have fun, annoying other people and getting into trouble. I did sit my Leaving Cert, but scraped through with 180 points. You might be surprised that I would admit to this, but what I'm trying to demonstrate is that people can achieve an amazing career and life even if they aren't academically gifted. I truly believe that you can do whatever you want in life as long as you put your mind to it.

In contrast to school, from a young age cooking gave me this feeling and light inside that I never want to lose. From the first day I stepped into that restaurant kitchen I felt I could express myself through food and cooking. It means so much to me – it's like my comfort zone, somewhere I can be creative, mixing flavours to make amazing food. And to keep things interesting, there's always something new to learn.

It took me a long time to decide what aspect of my cooking I wanted to concentrate on in this book. The reason I picked fast food was that growing up I loved takeaways. Many great nights in with my friends, watching football or just chilling out, were celebrated with so many different types of fast food. I was always trying to figure out how these dishes were made, and started experimenting with making them myself. I quickly discovered two problems. First, most takeaways are incredibly unhealthy, which I didn't want mine to be, and second, how could I make them taste exactly the same as the ones I ate growing up? Many nights of cooking at home (shout-out to the greatest dishwasher ever – my dad), tips and tricks picked up from working in some of the top restaurants in Ireland and from meeting home cooks, and a great deal of trial and error have led to the variety of recipes you'll find in this book.

There is something for everyone here. I don't know anyone who doesn't love a takeaway, but most of us hate the guilt afterwards of what we have put into our bodies. Now, with a bit of practice you can make your favourite takeaways at home, in a reasonable time and in a way that is ultimately much easier on the pocket and on your health. The recipes in the book are simple to make, with easily accessible and healthy ingredients. You'll find versions of many old favourites along with a few you might not expect but which are well worth trying. And since you've taken the healthy route with your main meal, I've also included a few of my favourite sweet treats for when you're feeling indulgent.

I've put my heart and soul into this book and I really hope you enjoy these recipes as much as I do.

Enjoy,

Adrian X

Author's Note: All the celsius temperatures in this book are for a fan oven. If using a conventional oven you will need to increase the temperature by 20 degrees.

COOKING TIPS
AND TRICKS

////////// ////////////////////////////////

Here are some cool little tricks and tips for you to try out in the kitchen that make life easy and relaxed while cooking.

1

If you put a teaspoon in your mouth while chopping or peeling an onion you won't get all teary-eyed and cry.

2

Remove the green part from the middle of garlic cloves as it causes stomach cramp.

3

Cook pasta separately for a minute less than the package instructions, then finish cooking it the rest of the way in the pan with your sauce, otherwise you'll have overcooked pasta.

4

After working with garlic or onions, rub your hands vigorously on your stainless-steel sink before washing them – this can help remove the smell.

5 If you find you need more oil in the pan when sautéing, add it in a stream along the edge of the pan so that by the time the oil reaches the ingredient being cooked, it will be heated.

6 When chopping herbs toss a bit of sea salt on the chopping board to stop them from flying around.

7 When cooking any type of meat remove it from the fridge at least 20–30 minutes before cooking to allow it to come to room temperature. Cooking meat from cold means the outside overcooks and the inside undercooks.

8 If you wet your fingers you'll be able to remove egg shell pieces a lot more easily.

9 When buying/cooking steak, lamb or pork, buy/cook with the fat on, as this provides most of the flavour. Only cut it off once it's cooked.

10 To get the most juice from a lime or lemon, roll it in the palm of your hand for 30 seconds before juicing.

A FEW BITS OF EQUIPMENT THAT WILL MAKE LIFE EASIER

- Good-quality food processor
- Liquidiser
- Stick blender
- Griddle pan
- Ovenproof frying pans
- Lidded pans
- Bamboo steamer
- Large, sturdy, high-sided roasting trays
- Large, non-stick baking trays
- Three good quality knives – chef's/paring/bread
- Wooden chopping boards
- Mixing bowls
- Colander
- Sieve
- Pestle and mortar
- Garlic crusher
- Tongs
- Fish slice
- Wooden spoons
- Slotted spoon
- Spatula
- Potato masher
- Speed peeler
- Box grater
- Microplane
- Measuring jugs
- Measuring spoons
- Scales
- Tin-opener
- Rolling pin
- Bottle-opener

And remember, own your kitchen! I've cooked in a lot of kitchens and bad organisation is common. It can stop you making meals quickly and efficiently. Clear out any clutter, such as magazines and random stuff. Anything you need for preparation should be close by and take some time to gather together the ingredients you need before you start cooking.

WHAT'S IN THE CUPBOARD?

//////////// ////////////////////////////////

OILS, VINEGARS, SAUCES, ETC.

Dijon mustard
Ketchup
Hot sauce (I like Frank's)
Camelina oil
Sesame oil
Olive oil
Balsamic vinegar
Red wine vinegar
White wine vinegar
Chicken/beef/vegetable stock
    cubes
Soy sauce
Sweet chilli sauce
Tinned tomatoes
Tomato purée
Honey
Worcestershire sauce
Coconut milk
Wine (red, white, or both)
Madeira wine (or brandy)

DRIED INGREDIENTS

Cardamom seeds
Chilli powder (mild and hot)
Cinnamon (ground and whole)
Cracked black pepper
Cumin
Curry powder (mild, medium or
    hot, depending on how spicy
    you like your curries)
Nutmeg
Garam masala
Garlic powder
Saffron
Sea salt
Smoked paprika
Star anise
Turmeric
Plain flour
Sugar (brown and granulated)

Keeping a well-stocked cupboard full of essentials is important and very useful. You will probably find that the majority of stuff I have listed here will already be in your cupboard, but you might not have found a use for it before. Because I spend so much time travelling to do demonstrations, my cupboard is a box in the boot of my car, but here's what's in it.

A FEW FACTS ABOUT DIETS AND NUTRITION

I believe in cooking everything from scratch and using the best ingredients you can afford, as by doing so you get the best nutritional value from your meals.

In a world where obesity is becoming a major problem, I get asked time and time again what the best diet is. My answer is none of them. They are all fads. Although you can lose weight at the start of a diet really quickly, that is because of the shock you've given your gut with the drastic change to your normal food intake. You body goes into shock mode and you lose weight. But to sustain a diet long-term is often impossible. You end up having a bad week and nine times out of ten you give up. And once you stop, all the weight that has fallen off very quickly comes back again, as you revert to your old eating habits. Moreover, the shock you've given your body can do long-term damage.

An important point to make here is that we do need some fat in our diets. Fat aids in digestion and gives you energy. Good natural full fats, such as cheese, milk, fat on meat, etc., are what we need to eat more of. Low-fat substitutes should be avoided at all costs, as these are stabilised with hidden sugars, and it is sugar that we need to be most careful of when we are eating.

Processed food is also full of sugar. Sugar is really hard to digest and excess sugar is converted by our liver into fatty acids and stored as fat, while excess blood sugar is also converted to fat, so over time we gain weight. The more processed bad sugars we eat, the more fat we store. It's the main reason why people become obese. The best sweetening options to use are sugars in natural forms, such as good quality honey, maple syrups, etc., but even with these we should be careful not to over-indulge.

The health of our gut is also very important for our overall health and well-being. The gut should have a broad range of both good and bad bacteria to keep it balanced and ensure that we remain healthy. To make sure that we have all the bacteria we need, it is important for us to eat a broad range of foods.

It's simple really. If we look at the way our grandparents used to cook, everything was made from scratch. Good quality creams and butters were used, yet they didn't have the same level of obesity problems that are so pervasive in today's society. The reason for this was that they didn't have the processed food option – takeaway and ready meals. Instead, they bought the best quality produce they could afford, cooked it from scratch and, of course, were a lot more active in their everyday lives.

So my advice would be, forget the diets. If you learn to cook your favourite meals yourself (it's super fun btw), using the best possible ingredients, you'll enjoy your food so much more, as well as being healthier and happier. Moreover you won't be stuck with a massive health bill in the future. Also do allow yourself a treat day now and again, and of course get out there and exercise!

INDIAN

CHICKEN TIKKA MASALA

Chicken tikka masala would be up there as one of my favourite mid-week meals. If I have the time I like to marinate the chicken overnight to ensure that I get an awesome flavour. I was disappointed the first time I had tikka masala from a takeaway as I found it dry. So I had to make it myself to really enjoy it.

/////////////// ///////////////////////////////////////

Serves 4

1 In a large bowl, mix the yoghurt, lemon zest, garam masala and cumin.

2 Slice the chicken so it can fit on skewers. I normally just cut each breast straight down the middle lengthways, so you are left with eight pieces.

3 Place one chicken piece on each skewer and marinate in the yoghurt mixture for as long as you wish (you can cook these straight away if you like).

4 Preheat the oven to 180ºC/350ºF/gas mark 4. Place the chicken skewers on a baking tray and bake in the oven for the 15–20 minutes, until fully cooked.

5 When the chicken is almost ready, make the sauce. Sweat the sliced onion, garlic and red chilli for 1–2 minutes over a medium heat. Add the garam masala and turmeric and sweat for 20–40 seconds, then add in the tomato purée and cook for 1–2 minutes.

6 Add in the coconut milk and then turn up the heat. Bring the sauce to the boil and simmer until the colour changes and the sauce thickens.

7 To finish the sauce add the coriander and season with salt to taste. Serve the chicken on a plate or platter and spoon the sauce over the chicken. I like to serve this with a side of mojito courgetti (see page 199) to really cool the heat of the masala.

6 heaped tablespoons natural yoghurt
zest of ½ lemon
1 tablespoon garam masala
1 tablespoon cumin
4 boneless chicken breasts

FOR THE SAUCE
1 onion, sliced
2 cloves of garlic, chopped
½ red chilli, chopped
1 tablespoon garam masala
1 tablespoon turmeric
2 tablespoons tomato purée
1 x 400ml tin of coconut milk
a handful of coriander, chopped
sea salt

BUTTER CHICKEN

Probably one of the best-known Indian dishes after tikka masala. My first time having it was in Greenwich Market in London and from then on I was hooked.

///////////////   ////////////////////////////////////

Serves 4

1   Place all the ingredients for the marinade in a bowl, add the whole chicken thighs and toss until completely coated. Cover and leave to marinate for a while, preferably overnight.

2   Heat a large griddle pan over a high heat and cook the chicken until it has deep char marks. Then place the chicken into a large casserole dish over the heat and continue to cook, basting with the melted butter and lemon juice, until it is fully cooked. Remove from the pot and set aside.

3   For the sauce add the butter to the casserole dish along with the olive oil to stop it from burning. When the butter has melted, add in the cardamom pods and the onion. Cook for 3–4 minutes until the onion is softened and slightly browned.

4   Add in the garlic, ginger and chilli and continue to cook for 2 minutes. Then stir through the garam masala, cumin, coriander, sweet paprika and tomato purée.

5   Lower the heat and, stirring continuously, slowly add the cream until well combined. Bring to a low simmer and season with sea salt to taste. Stir through the chicken and cook until it's warmed through. Serve with basmati rice and/or naan breads.

500g boneless, skinless chicken thighs
50g butter, melted
juice of 1 lemon

FOR THE MARINADE
150ml plain yoghurt
1 large thumb-sized piece of ginger, finely grated
3 cloves of garlic, finely grated
1 tablespoon garam masala
1 teaspoon cumin
2 teaspoons ground coriander

FOR THE SAUCE
50g butter
2 tablespoons olive oil
4 green cardamom pods
1 onion, finely chopped
5 cloves of garlic, finely chopped
1 large thumb-sized piece of ginger, finely grated
1 green chilli, finely chopped
1 tablespoon garam masala
1 teaspoon cumin
2 teaspoons ground coriander
1 teaspoon sweet paprika
4 tablespoons tomato purée
200ml double cream
sea salt

CHICKEN
CURRY

This recipe was one of the first I learned back in the day. It hasn't changed from day one and is another of my favourite mid-week meals.

//////////////   //////////////////////////////

Serves 4

1 Preheat the oven to 180ºC/350ºF/gas mark 4.

2 Place the chicken on a baking sheet, season with some salt, drizzle with a little oil, then cook in the oven for around 20–25 minutes, until cooked through.

3 Heat some oil in a wide saucepan over a medium heat, then sweat the onion, garlic and lemon grass for 2–3 minutes. Reduce the heat and add in the curry powder and tomato purée. Cook for another 30 seconds, stirring constantly. Finish the sauce by adding the coconut milk, ginger, sweet chilli sauce and mango chutney. Stir well then taste and season to your liking with salt and black pepper.

4 Meanwhile, steam the broccoli for 3 minutes, then cook in the sauce for another 2 minutes. When the chicken is ready, slice it up on a chopping board and add the pieces to the sauce.

5 Now you are ready to serve. I love serving this in the middle of the table on a platter with a big bowl of rice for everyone to help themselves.

4 chicken breasts
sea salt
olive oil
1 onion, sliced
2 cloves of garlic, finely chopped
1 stick of lemon grass, chopped
2 teaspoons mild curry powder or garam masala
100g tomato purée
1 x 400ml tin of coconut milk
a thumb-sized piece of ginger, grated
2 tablespoons sweet chilli sauce
2 tablespoons mango chutney
freshly ground black pepper
200g sprouting broccoli

LAMB SKEWERS WITH TAMARIND SAUCE

Tamarind has a unique sweet, tart flavour, making this sauce very distinctive. The recipe can be made with any other meat, but I like the lamb version. Tamarind has many health benefits – it's full of iron and magnesium and can ease stomach discomfort.

/////////// //////////////////////////

Serves 2

1 To make the sauce, combine the ingredients in a small saucepan and place onto a hob over a medium heat to dissolve the ingredients in the water. Then boil the sauce hard, stirring constantly, for 3–5 minutes until it becomes thick and syrupy. Refrigerate until completely cool, then reserve half as a table sauce and use the other half to brush on the lamb while cooking.

2 Using your hands, combine the lamb, coriander, salt and pepper in a bowl, then squish down flat and divide into four equal portions. Take one portion of the lamb mix and, with wet hands, form it on a damp chopping board into a sausage-shaped roll around a skewer. If you are using wooden rather than metal skewers, make sure you soak them in advance for about 20 minutes. Repeat with the other three portions.

3 Preheat your grill to a high heat. Place the lamb kebabs onto a tray lined with tinfoil and brush the uppermost side with the tamarind sauce. Slide under the grill to cook, turning the skewers with tongs frequently to ensure even cooking. After each turning, brush with the tamarind sauce. These should take about 6–8 minutes to cook. Brush them with the sauce one last time as you remove them to a serving platter.

4 Serve them up with the remaining tamarind sauce, heated or cold, and enjoy. These go great with sticky coconut rice (see page 190).

400g ground lamb
1 teaspoon ground coriander
1 teaspoon sea salt
1 teaspoon freshly ground black pepper

FOR THE SAUCE
200ml water
2 tablespoons tamarind paste
2 tablespoons brown cane sugar
1½ tablespoons soy sauce
1½ tablespoons date molasses

TANDOORI HALIBUT WITH RAITA

My first memory of halibut is a whole fish that was the same height as me, which we had delivered while I was working in the MacNean House restaurant. Three of us had to lift it, but I got to fillet it. Here's a tandoori version with a classic raita. This paste also works great with chicken.

//////////// //////////////////////////////

Serves 4

1   To make the paste, start by toasting the cumin and coriander seeds in a frying pan until fragrant. Tip them into a pestle and mortar and grind into a powder. Mix in all the other ingredients and stir until you have a smooth paste.

2   Preheat the oven to 200ºC/400ºF/gas mark 6.

3   Place the halibut fillets on a plate. Mix the curry paste with one tablespoon of olive oil and the sugar. Add the yoghurt and stir well. Coat the halibut fillets with the spiced yoghurt mixture and set aside.

4   To make the raita, cut the cucumbers lengthways, using a vegetable peeler, into long wide strips, avoiding the seeds in the middle. Mix with the yoghurt, chopped mint and lime juice to taste.

5   Heat an ovenproof pan over a medium to high heat and add the remaining olive oil. Scrape off and reserve the excess marinade from the fish. When the pan is hot, place the halibut fillets into it. Sear for 1–1½ minutes on each side until golden brown.

6   Spoon the reserved marinade over the fish and place the pan in the oven for a few minutes to finish cooking the fish. Spoon the raita onto warm plates and then serve the halibut on top. Drizzle with the pan juices and serve with some onion bhajis (see page 189).

FOR THE PASTE
1 teaspoon cumin seeds
1 teaspoon coriander seeds
2 teaspoons garam masala
2 teaspoons sweet paprika
1 teaspoon hot chilli powder
juice of ½ lemon
2 tablespoons olive oil
1 teaspoon salt
½ teaspoon turmeric
1 tablespoon tomato purée
3 cloves of garlic, crushed
a large piece of root ginger,
   finely grated

FOR THE HALIBUT
4 halibut fillets (about 150g
   each), skinned
3 tablespoons olive oil
1 teaspoon caster sugar
3 tablespoons natural
   yoghurt

FOR THE RAITA
2 cucumbers, peeled
3–4 tablespoons natural
   yoghurt
mint leaves, chopped
juice of ½ lime

LAMB SHANK ROGAN JOSH

The inspiration for this recipe came from a time when my lecturer Gabriel McSharry made his incredible rogan josh in college. I loved the spices and felt they gave the ordinary lamb shank a complete lift. Here is my take on his recipe. Cheers Gabriel.

Serves 4

1 Preheat the oven to 180ºC/350ºF/gas mark 4.

2 Heat the oil in a frying pan over a high heat and sweat the cinnamon, cardamom, fennel and cumin seeds and bay leaves in it. Then add the onions, ginger and garlic, and fry, stirring constantly, until they turn golden, using a pinch of salt to help them sweat.

3 Add the ground cumin, coriander and chilli and continue to stir, adding two tablespoons of cold water to prevent the spices from burning.

4 Add the tomato purée and the chopped tomatoes with the sugar to balance the acidity.

5 Gradually add the yoghurt and stir in to the mixture. Keep stirring until all the yoghurt has incorporated into the sauce and making sure the oil has not separated.

6 Sear the lamb in some oil in a frying pan on a high heat, ensuring that it is sealed and browned all over.

7 Place the meat in an oven roasting tray, then pour over the sauce, cover with foil and roast in the oven for 3 hours, until the meat is tender.

8 Remove from the oven, mix the garam masala into the sauce with a spoon, and adjust the seasoning with sea salt. Spoon the lamb shanks into bowls and ladle over that amazing sauce. Finally sprinkle with the chopped coriander and enjoy with a side of your choice. I love serving this with some mashed potato or sticky rice.

4 tablespoons olive oil +
extra for searing
2 cinnamon sticks
5 cardamom pods
1 teaspoon fennel seeds
1 teaspoon cumin seeds
1–2 bay leaves
2 onions, sliced
1 tablespoon grated ginger
1 tablespoon chopped garlic
sea salt
1 teaspoon ground cumin
1 teaspoon ground
coriander
2 teaspoons chilli powder
2 tablespoons tomato purée
2 x 400g tins of chopped
tomatoes
1 tablespoon sugar
4 tablespoons Greek
yoghurt
4 lamb shanks, excess fat
removed
1 tablespoon garam masala
2 tablespoons chopped
coriander

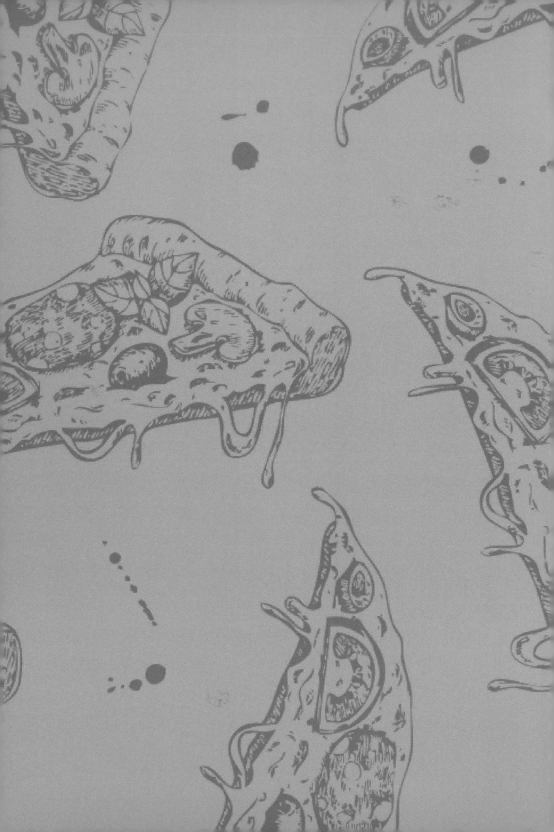

ITALIAN

GOATS CHEESE, CARAMELISED RED ONION AND BASIL PESTO PIZZA

This is the classic Italian recipe, but with my own spin on it. The wild blackberry balsamic vinegar, if you can get it, really cuts nicely through the goats cheese. The pesto from this recipe can also be used for pasta, or to flavour and marinate roast lamb.

/////////// /////////////////////////////

Serves 4

1 Place the flour and salt onto a clean work surface and make a well in the middle. In a jug, mix the yeast and olive oil into the water and leave for a few minutes, then pour into the well.

2 Using a fork, bring the flour in gradually from the sides and swirl it into the liquid. Keep mixing, drawing larger amounts of flour in, and when it all starts to come together, work the rest of the flour in with flour-dusted hands. Knead and work until you have a smooth, springy dough.

3 Place the dough into a flour-dusted bowl, cover with a damp cloth or cling film, and allow to double in size in a warm room. This normally takes about an hour.

4 Remove the dough and knead it for a small bit to push out the air. This is called knocking it back. You can either use it straight away or cover it in cling film and refrigerate or freeze.

5 Peel and halve the red onion. Slice it as thinly as you can and then place into a bowl. Sprinkle with the sea salt and pour in the balsamic vinegar. Now with your fingers scrunch the red onion in the vinegar and set aside until needed. This will last up to three weeks in a jar in your fridge.

6 To make the pesto, place all the ingredients, excluding the olive oil, into a food processor and blitz for a minute or two, then slowly pour in the olive oil, continuing to blitz until blended.

500g wholemeal flour
1 teaspoon sea salt
1 x 7g sachet of dried yeast
2 tablespoons olive oil
325ml lukewarm water

FOR THE TOPPING
1 red onion
a pinch of sea salt
30ml wild blackberry balsamic vinegar (ordinary balsamic vinegar will do)
100g Boilie goats cheese (or any other crumbly kind)
5–6 small basil leaves to garnish

FOR THE PESTO
1 large bunch of fresh basil (around 2 handfuls)
60g pine nuts, toasted
60g Parmesan
squeeze of lemon juice
1 teaspoon salt and pepper
150ml olive oil (half extra virgin, half normal)

7 Prepare the dough by pulling off a piece and rolling it to whatever size you like. You can either use a rolling pin dusted with flour, or you can go wild and spin the dough with your hands to flatten it.

8 Spread with a layer of pesto, then add the red onion and crumble over the goats cheese. Place the pizza onto a flour-dusted tray or onto a heated pizza stone or granite slab, and bake in a preheated oven at 240ºC/475ºF/gas mark 9 for 4–5 minutes, until the dough is puffed up and golden. I like to finish the pizza with baby basil leaves and an extra drizzle of balsamic vinegar.

SPAGHETTI ALLE VONGOLE

Spaghetti alle vongole is the Italian for spaghetti with clams. I tried it for the first time on holidays in Cannes in France as a nine-year-old, where they served it in take-out containers and you ate it on the go. I loved the sweetness that the clams had. Use sustainable clams for this one if you can – you can ask your fishmonger for these.

/////////////////   /////////////////////////////////////

Serves 4

1   Put a pan of water on to boil that is big enough to hold the spaghetti. While that is coming to the boil, sort through your cleaned clams and if there are any that aren't tightly closed, give them a sharp tap. If they don't close, throw them away.

2   Put a large pan with a lid on a high heat and let it heat up. In the meantime, finely slice the parsley stalks, then put them to one side and roughly chop the leaves. Peel and chop the garlic, quarter the tomatoes and get your wine ready.

3   Add the pasta to the boiling water with a good pinch of salt and cook according to packet instructions until al dente.

4   About 5 minutes before your pasta is due to be ready, get ready to start on the sauce – you'll have to be quick about this, so no messing around! Put enough extra virgin olive oil into the hot pan to cover the bottom and add the garlic, parsley stalks and a good pinch of salt and pepper.

5   Add in the chilli and the tomatoes. Stir everything around constantly and just as the garlic starts to colour, tip in the clams and pour in the wine. It will splutter and steam, so give everything a good shake and put the lid on. After about 3–4 minutes the clams will start to open – keep shuffling the pan around until all of them have opened. Take the pan off the heat. Get rid of

400g spaghetti
1kg small clams, scrubbed clean
1 small bunch of fresh flat-leaf parsley
4 cloves of garlic
10 cherry tomatoes
250ml white wine
sea salt
extra virgin olive oil
freshly ground black pepper
1 red chilli, finely chopped
2 knobs of butter
juice of ½ lemon

any clams that haven't opened. Stir in the butter and lemon juice.

6 By now your pasta should be just about perfect. Drain and add it to the pan of clams along with the parsley leaves and an extra drizzle of the olive oil. Stir or toss for a further 1–2 minutes to let the beautiful juices from the clams absorb into the pasta, then serve right away.

TOMATO, MOZZARELLA AND BASIL PAN PIZZA

Did you know that Americans eat 100 acres of pizza a day, or around 350 slices of pizza a second? This recipe is an incredibly simple way of cooking pizza, taking the time and pressure out of it. Just don't tell the Italians!

/////////// ///////////////////////////

Serves 4

1 Preheat the oven to 200ºC/400ºF/gas mark 6.

2 In a bowl mix the self-raising flour, water and sea salt with a fork. Then knead it on a work surface with your hands for 2–3 minutes until smooth.

3 Cut the dough in half and, using a rolling pin, roll each half out into a pizza base on a floured work surface.

4 Place each base into a frying pan on the hob over a low heat to warm for 30 seconds to 1 minute.

5 To make the tomato sauce, mix the passata, vinegar and honey, then chop some of the basil into it and stir. Spread the tomato sauce over the pizza bases then top with the mozzarella and ham.

6 Bake in the oven for 4–5 minutes until crispy and cooked. Serve sliced on a board, with the rest of the basil leaves sprinkled over the top.

1½ cups self-raising flour
½ cup water
a pinch of sea salt
½ x 600g jar of tomato passata
1 tablespoon balsamic vinegar
1 tablespoon honey
a handful of fresh basil
1 ball of mozzarella, torn into pieces
8 slices of Parma/Serrano ham

PIZZA ROLLS

Pizza rolls are incredibly simple to make and delicious. Stick them in your lunch box for the ultimate quick lunch.

//////////////// ////////////////////////////////

Serves 6

1   Preheat the oven to 180ºC/350ºF/gas mark 4.

2   For the first topping mix the passata, balsamic vinegar and honey together in a bowl. Spoon this sauce onto one of the sheets of puff pastry, spreading it to cover the pastry, then scatter the cheddar over the top. Roll the sheet of puff pastry up to the end and then cut into slices 2–3cm thick. Place them spaced out on a tray lined with parchment paper.

3   For the second topping, slice the red onions thinly and then fry them off in a little olive oil over a medium heat until soft. Add in the balsamic vinegar and honey and allow to caramelise. Spread the basil pesto over the second sheet of puff pastry and then top it with the red onion marmalade and grated Parmesan. Roll the sheet of puff pastry up to the end and then cut 2–3cm slices. Place them spaced out on a tray lined with parchment paper.

4   Brush both trays of pizza rolls with egg wash.

5   Bake the rolls for 15–20 minutes. Serve on a wooden board, accompanied by the balsamic vinegar and olive oil mixed to make an amazing dip.

2 sheets of puff pastry
1 egg, beaten

TOPPING NUMBER 1
250ml tomato passata
2 tablespoons balsamic vinegar
2 tablespoons honey
2–3 handfuls of grated cheddar

TOPPING NUMBER 2
2 red onions
olive oil
2 tablespoons balsamic vinegar
2 tablespoons honey
4 tablespoons basil pesto
2–3 handfuls of grated Parmesan

TO SERVE (OPTIONAL)
100ml good quality olive oil
3–4 tablespoons balsamic vinegar

PIZZA CALZONE

The classic calzone is normally stuffed with salami or ham, mozzarella, ricotta and Parmesan or pecorino cheese, as well as an egg, but here I've used my favourite filling combination. Be careful when tucking into these incredible parcels as I have burnt my tongue on a few occasions.

///////////////   ///////////////////////////////////

Serves 4

1 To make the dough, sieve the flour and salt onto a clean work surface and make a well in the middle. In a jug, mix the yeast, sugar and oil into the water and leave for a few minutes, then pour into the well. Using a fork, bring the flour in gradually from the sides and swirl it into the liquid. Keep mixing, drawing larger amounts of flour in, and when it all starts to come together, work the rest of the flour in with flour-dusted hands. Knead and work until you have a smooth, springy dough.

2 Place the dough into a flour-dusted bowl, cover with a damp cloth or cling film, and allow to double in size in a warm room. This normally takes about an hour.

3 When the dough has risen, remove it from the bowl and knead it for a small bit to push out the air. This is called knocking it back. You can either use it straight away or cover it in cling film and refrigerate or freeze.

4 For the filling, place a frying pan over a high heat, add a good glug of oil and sweat off the bacon, onion and thyme. Once cooked, add the tomato passata, balsamic vinegar and sugar, and season with some sea salt if needed. Bring the sauce to the boil and simmer until thick. Allow to cool.

5 Preheat the oven to 240ºC/475ºF/gas mark 9.

FOR THE DOUGH
500g strong white bread flour + extra for dusting
1 teaspoon sea salt
1 x 7g sachet of dried yeast
1 teaspoon caster sugar
2 tablespoons olive oil
325ml lukewarm water

FOR THE FILLING
olive oil
4 streaky smoked bacon rashers, cut into lardons
½ onion, diced
2 sprigs of thyme, finely chopped
5 heaped tablespoons tomato passata
1 tablespoon balsamic vinegar
1 tablespoon sugar
sea salt
100g Parmesan, grated
100g mozzarella, broken up

6 Pull off a piece of dough about the size of a tennis ball and roll into a ball. It should be around 4cm in diameter if you are very accurate. Roll the dough out with a rolling pin or flatten with your hands until you've reached the size of a large pancake.

7 Place about 2 heaped tablespoons of the filling in the centre of the dough and top with some of the Parmesan and mozzarella.

8 Fold the dough over on itself across the filling and crimp it at the edges like a Cornish pasty. Repeat this until you have four calzones.

9 Place the calzones onto a flour-dusted tray or onto a heated pizza stone or a granite slab and bake for 5–6 minutes until the dough is puffed up and golden.

PROSCIUTTO
CHICKEN

A simple way of adding lovely flavour to your chicken breasts. This is a popular mid-week meal in our home in Cavan. Sometimes you'd swear we were Italian!

///////////// //////////////////////////////////

Serves 4

1 Preheat the oven to 180ºC/350ºF/gas mark 4.

2 Put two tablespoons of olive oil in a saucepan over a medium heat and wilt the spinach. Season with a pinch of sea salt, then place onto some kitchen paper to soak up any moisture.

3 Slice into the side of each chicken breast to make a flap and then stuff them with equal portions of the cheese and wilted spinach. Wrap each chicken breast with two slices of the ham and then bake in a roasting tin for 25 minutes in the oven.

4 Put two more tablespoons of olive oil into the saucepan and cook the mushrooms over a high heat until they are soft. Make sure you get a nice colour on the mushrooms. Add the thyme and beef stock, and reduce by half over a really high heat. This normally takes 1–2 minutes. Finally, add the cream and season with salt and pepper. Cook for a further 2 minutes until the sauce has thickened.

5 When the chicken is cooked pour over the sauce and serve. I like to serve with a side of sticky coconut rice (see page 190).

olive oil
2 handfuls of spinach leaves
sea salt
4 chicken breasts
1 ball of mozzarella cheese, sliced
8 slices of prosciutto ham
8 chestnut mushrooms, sliced
2 sprigs of thyme, finely chopped
200ml beef stock (stock cube and water)
200ml cream
freshly ground black pepper

RISOTTO

I know this is Italian, but I love a small portion of risotto as a tapas meal when having guests over. A tub of this risotto on the go also makes an amazing lunch. You can make a big batch and freeze the extra in portions in freezer bags.

/////////////////// ///////////////////////////////////////

Serves 4

1   Make the stock in a saucepan. Peel and finely chop the onion and garlic, trim and finely chop the celery. Finely grate the Parmesan.

2   In a separate pan, heat the oil and a tablespoon of butter over a low heat, then add the onions, garlic and celery and fry gently for about 15 minutes, or until softened but not coloured.

3   Add the rice and turn up the heat to medium – the rice will begin to lightly fry, so keep stirring it. After 1 minute it will look slightly translucent. Add the wine and keep stirring – it will smell fantastic. Any harsh alcohol flavours will evaporate and leave the rice with a tasty essence.

4   Once the wine has cooked into the rice, add your first ladle of hot stock and a good pinch of sea salt. Turn the heat down to a simmer so the rice doesn't cook too quickly on the outside.

5   Keep adding ladlefuls of stock, stirring and almost massaging the creamy starch out of the rice, allowing each ladleful to be absorbed before adding the next. Carry on adding stock until the rice is soft but with a slight bite. Don't forget to check the seasoning carefully. If you run out of stock before the rice is cooked, add some boiling water. (The stock can reduce quicker in different-sized pans and on different heats so you may or may not need the extra water.)

6   Remove the pan from the heat, add another tablespoon of butter and the Parmesan, then stir well.

1.1 litres stock (chicken, fish or vegetable)
1 large onion
2 cloves of garlic
4 sticks of celery
90g Parmesan
2 tablespoons olive oil
unsalted butter
400g Arborio rice
2 wine glasses of dry white wine
sea salt

7 Place a lid on the pan and allow to sit for 2 minutes – this is the most important part of making the perfect risotto, as this is when it becomes creamy and oozy like it should be. Eat it as soon as possible, while the risotto retains its beautiful texture, or cool it down nice and quick and reheat for the ultimate lunch.

BASIL PESTO LINGUINE

A classic fast food and something that you can whip up in minutes. The ingredient amounts here make enough for this recipe, but you can multiply the amounts and store the pesto in a jar in the fridge. It keeps for up to three weeks. If you are using bought basil pesto just make sure that it is bright green. When pre-made pestos have been sitting on shelves for months they turn a much darker colour and just aren't as nice. I highly recommend Moran's Homestore Pesto from Ballinagh, Cavan, if you can get it.

//////////////////   //

Serves 2

1 Cook the pasta according to the packet instructions.

2 Meanwhile, blend together the pine nuts, garlic and basil in a pestle and mortar. Add the sea salt and olive oil. Then stir in the grated Parmesan.

3 Mix together the cooked pasta and the pesto and enjoy.

200g linguine pasta or spaghetti
a handful of toasted pine nuts
2 cloves of garlic
2 handfuls of fresh basil
a pinch of sea salt
5 tablespoons olive oil
50g Parmesan cheese

BURGERS AND 'DOGS

THE CLASSIC CHEESEBURGER

Burger is actually a stripped name. The actual name is hamburger, derived from Hamburg steaks, which were introduced to the USA by German immigrants.

/////////// //////////////////////////

Serves 4

1 Combine the minced beef, Dijon mustard, Worcestershire sauce, garlic, ketchup, thyme, salt and pepper in a large bowl and mix until everything is evenly combined. Divide into four and shape into patties.

2 Place a large pan on a medium to high heat and add the oil. Fry the pancetta for 2–3 minutes on either side until nice and crisp, then set aside.

3 Reduce the heat to medium, place the burger patties in the pan, and fry for 6 minutes on either side or until cooked through and browned. Once cooked, top with the cheese and cover with a steel bowl or lid for 2–3 minutes until the cheese is oozing and melted.

4 Make your spicy mayo by mixing the mayonnaise and hot sauce – how much you use depends on how hot you like it. And don't forget to toast your buns.

5 Place the bottom of the toasted bun onto a plate, smear with a dollop of the spicy mayo, top with a burger, some of the crisp pancetta and rocket, followed by the burger bun top. If you are using ketchup don't forget to put your favourite on and tuck in.

600g beef mince
1 teaspoon Dijon mustard
1 teaspoon Worcestershire sauce
2 cloves of garlic, minced
1 tablespoon ketchup
1 teaspoon thyme leaves, finely chopped
2 tablespoons sea salt
1 teaspoon cracked black pepper
2 tablespoons olive oil
8 slices of pancetta
75g Gruyère cheese, sliced
4 seeded buns
50g rocket
ketchup (optional)

FOR THE SPICY MAYO
75g mayonnaise
1–2 tablespoons hot sauce

THE PIMPED-UP BURGER

If you like eggs you will love this burger. The egg bakes in the centre of the bun and also toasts the bun at the same time.

Serves 4

1   Preheat the oven to 170ºC/325ºF/gas mark 3.

2   Mix the mince, sea salt, breadcrumbs, egg yolks, ginger and sweet chilli sauce in a large bowl. Split the mixture into four pieces and shape into patties.

3   Heat some oil in a frying pan over a medium heat and cook the patties until they are golden and crispy on each side.

4   While the patties are cooking, use a ring cutter to cut out a ring from the top of each of the burger buns. Put these on a baking tray lined with parchment paper and crack an egg into the hole in the middle of each. Bake the buns with the eggs in the oven for 5–8 minutes. If you like your egg runny take it out after 5 minutes. If you like it well cooked, leave it in for the full 8 minutes.

5   Once the burgers are cooked, grate the cheese over them.

6   Now it's time to build your burger. Spread a layer of mayonnaise on the bottom part of the burger bun, then add the burger with cheese, blob some sweet chilli sauce on top, and top off with the eggy bun. Delicious!

570g beef mince
2 good pinches of sea salt
100g breadcrumbs
4 eggs + 2 egg yolks
a small piece of ginger, grated
2 tablespoons sweet chilli sauce + extra for topping
olive oil
4 of your favourite buns
400g smoked cheddar
mayonnaise

THE TURKEY BURGER

This turkey burger really is full of flavour. However, be careful not to overcook, as these burgers can dry out very quickly.

Serves 4

1 To make the pickled onion, combine the ingredients in a bowl and leave aside until the burgers are cooked.

2 Mix together the minced turkey, lemon zest, shallots, ginger, garlic, salt and coriander in a large bowl until combined. Divide into four and shape into patties. A good tip, when forming your patties, is to wet your hands to stop the meat sticking to them.

3 Drizzle some oil into a pan on a high heat and place the patties onto the pan. Cook for 8–10 minutes, turning down the heat every now and again to make sure you don't overcolour them.

4 Once cooked, top with the cheese and cover with a steel bowl or lid for 2–3 minutes until the cheese is oozing and melted.

5 Add the turkey bacon to the pan and cook for 3 minutes, or until cooked through.

6 For the burger sauce, combine all the ingredients and mix well. Once this is ready add the lettuce and stir through the sauce so it is fully coated.

7 To assemble your burger, place some of the lettuce and burger sauce on the bottom of each bun, then add the turkey burger and place the turkey bacon on top. Finally top with some of the pickled onion and the top of the bun.

600g minced turkey
zest of 1 lemon
2 shallots, finely diced
1 thumb-sized piece of ginger, grated
2 cloves of garlic, finely diced
a pinch of sea salt
1 bunch of coriander, finely chopped (alternatively use parley or thyme)
olive oil
4 slices of white cheddar (or cheese of your choice)
4 slices of turkey bacon
¼ head of iceberg lettuce, shredded
4 wholegrain buns

FOR THE PICKLED ONION
1 red onion, finely sliced
a pinch of sea salt
4 tablespoons white wine vinegar

FOR THE BURGER SAUCE
3 tablespoons mayonnaise
1 tablespoon Worcester sauce
1 teaspoon Tabasco sauce
juice of 1 lemon

BUTTERMILK CHICKEN BURGER

This is my spin on the McChicken sandwich. The buttermilk tenderises the chicken and gives an amazing crunch to the outside of the meat.

/////////// ///////////////////////////

Serves 2

1 First, make the marinade. In a bowl smash up the garlic cloves, then add the lemon zest, the thyme sprigs and the buttermilk. Place the butterflied chicken into it and allow to marinate for as long as you can.

2 Once the chicken has marinated, mix 2 pinches of sea salt with the flour, chilli powder and garlic powder in another bowl. Dip each of the chicken breasts into this flour mix and make sure they are coated thoroughly.

3 Heat a pot filled with about 1–2cm of oil over a high heat. When the oil is hot, place the chicken into the pot and fry until crispy on both sides and fully cooked through. Alternatively you can drizzle the chicken with oil, place on a baking tray and bake in a preheated oven at 200ºC/400ºF/gas mark 6 for 15 minutes.

4 Once the chicken is ready, place it onto some kitchen paper to drain and sprinkle with a little sea salt.

5 Now build up your burger. Spoon some mayonnaise onto the wholemeal bun and then place the crispy chicken in the centre. You can top this with sliced tomatoes, a little gem lettuce or, for a super treat, some crispy smoked streaky bacon.

4 cloves of garlic
zest of 1 lemon
3 sprigs of thyme
300ml buttermilk
2 chicken breasts, butterflied
sea salt
250g flour
1 teaspoon chilli powder
1–2 teaspoon garlic powder
rapeseed oil
low-fat mayonnaise
2 wholemeal burger buns

HOMEMADE CHILLI DOGS

Chilli dogs are a type of street food that most people would probably associate almost immediately with America. Basically they are a hot dog with some sort of meat sauce on top. Kids go crazy for this recipe.

//////////// ////////////////////////////////

Serves 2

1 First make the quick chilli con carne. Heat a saucepan over a medium heat, add a dash of oil and, once hot, sweat the onion for 4–5 minutes, then add the garlic and fry for another minute until soft. Add the cumin seeds and stir over a medium heat for 1–2 minutes until aromatic. Add the chilli powder and mix well.

2 Turn up the heat and add another dash of oil to the pan. Season the mince, then add to the pan and fry over a high heat for 6–8 minutes, stirring well to break it up. When it is lightly browned, add the Worcestershire sauce, turn down the heat and add the tomato purée, cooking for 1–2 minutes.

3 Add the chopped tomatoes, sugar and oregano along with a pinch of pepper. Bring to a simmer, cover and simmer gently for 20 minutes, stirring frequently.

4 Meanwhile, prepare the caramelised onions. Heat a small frying pan over a low heat and add a dash of olive oil. Add the onions with a good pinch of salt and gently sweat for 10–15 minutes until completely softened and turning a rich golden colour. (Don't increase the heat to speed up this process as you'll end up with burnt onions.)

5 Once the onions are golden and really soft, add the honey and balsamic vinegar. Increase the heat to medium and allow to caramelise gently. Cook for about 5 minutes until the liquid is reduced and the onions are nice and sticky. Taste and adjust the seasoning as necessary.

2 large Frankfurter-style hot dog sausages
2 wholegrain hot dog buns
50g cheddar cheese, crumbled or grated
1 spring onion, trimmed and finely chopped (optional)

FOR THE CHILLI
olive oil, for frying
1 small onion, peeled and finely diced
2 cloves of garlic, peeled and finely chopped
½ teaspoon cumin seeds
½–1 teaspoon mild chilli powder, to taste
300g minced beef
sea salt
1 teaspoon Worcestershire sauce
2 teaspoons tomato purée
1 × 400g tin chopped tomatoes
a pinch of caster sugar
½ teaspoon dried oregano
freshly ground black pepper

FOR THE CARAMELISED ONIONS
olive oil, for frying
2 red onions, peeled and finely sliced
sea salt
2 tablespoons honey
1 tablespoon balsamic vinegar

6 When ready to serve, boil or griddle the sausages for 6 minutes or until heated through. Remove and drain if necessary. Divide the caramelised onions between the opened hot dog buns. Top with the cooked sausage and a generous spoonful or two of chilli con carne. Top with the cheese and finish with a sprinkling of spring onion.

PORK SLIDERS

A slider is a mini burger. These little bites are delicious and are a real winner with kids. I'd normally eat three or four of them. This is real American diner-style food at its best.

///////////// /////////////////////////////

Serves 2 or 4 small ones

1 First mix the mince and smoked bacon with a pinch of salt and cracked black pepper. Make into eight little meatballs, then flatten with the palm of your hand to form patties.

2 Heat some oil in a frying pan on a high heat and cook the patties on each side for 2 minutes, then turn down the heat and finish for another 3 minutes on each side.

3 Meanwhile add a glug of oil to another pan and sweat the onion and garlic until soft over a medium to high heat, then add in the brown sugar. Stir until it has dissolved to form a dark caramel. This usually takes about 30 seconds to 1 minute on a high heat.

4 Add the smoked paprika, ketchup and Worcestershire sauce and heat through for 30 seconds.

5 To assemble the little sliders put some rocket on the bottom of each bun, topped with a burger, a slice of smoked cheese, some of the homemade barbecue sauce and then the top of the bun. Secure it all together with a skewer and enjoy.

400g pork mince
2 smoked bacon rashers, diced
sea salt and freshly ground black pepper
olive oil

FOR THE BARBECUE SAUCE
½ onion, diced
1 clove of garlic, roughly chopped
1 heaped tablespoon brown sugar
1 tablespoon smoked paprika
4 tablespoons tomato ketchup
1 tablespoon Worcestershire sauce

FOR SERVING
8 slider baps, halved
4 slices of smoked cheese, halved
Rocket leaves for serving

CHINESE

CRISPY SALT AND CHILLI CHICKEN

The ultimate snack. I love the spicy, salty flavour this has. I used to choose this so often when ordering Chinese food. It can be used as a starter or served as a side with a main.

/////////// ///////////////////////////////

Serves 2

1 Preheat the oven to 180ºC/350ºF/gas mark 4.

2 Whisk the two eggs in a bowl with the milk.

3 In a separate bowl or on a plate, mix the breadcrumbs with the garlic granules and chilli powder.

4 Peel and slice the onion nice and thin.

5 Slice the chicken breasts thinly and place into the whisked egg mixture along with the sliced onions, then dip them into the breadcrumbs in batches.

6 Place onto a baking tray greased with coconut or olive oil and bake in the oven for 15–20 minutes.

7 Serve sprinkled with chopped red chilli and sea salt to taste.

2 medium eggs
100ml milk
200g wholemeal breadcrumbs
1 teaspoon garlic granules
1 teaspoon chilli powder
1 onion
2 chicken breasts
coconut or olive oil for greasing
1–2 red chillies
sea salt

CRISPY SALT AND CHILLI WINGS

Here is my spin on the classic Chinese salt and chilli wings. These are by far my favourite kind of chicken wing. Serve as a nice starter to warm up the stomach, or go all out and have them with some Parmesan fries (see page 184) as a main.

//////////// //////////////////////////

Serves 4 as a starter, 2 as a main

1 Preheat the oven to 190ºC/375ºF/gas mark 5.

2 In a large bowl mix together the cornflour, garlic powder and chilli powder with a spoon. Then place the chicken wings into the cornflour mix and coat them all over.

3 Lay the wings onto a baking tray, spoon over the coconut oil and roast for 45 minutes until golden and crispy.

4 To make the dip, mix the mayonnaise and harissa paste together in a bowl. Finely chop the garlic, or crush it, and mix into the mayonnaise. Now squeeze in the lemon juice and mix really well.

5 Once the wings are cooked, sprinkle them with a good amount of sea salt to season. Slice the chillies (I like to keep the seeds but you can remove them if you don't like these too hot) and sprinkle over the wings.

6 Serve with the incredible dip, tuck in and enjoy.

150g cornflour
½ teaspoon garlic powder
½ teaspoon chilli powder
24 chicken wings
2 tablespoons coconut oil, melted
sea salt
2 red chillies

FOR THE DIP
3 heaped tablespoons mayonnaise
4 teaspoons harissa paste
1 clove of garlic
juice of ½ lemon

CRISPY DUCK NOODLES

Here's my take on the popular Chinese takeaway dish. The crispier the duck is, the better. Once you have the duck ready you can put this dish together in 5 minutes. If you don't have the time to cook the duck, I recommend buying pre-cooked confit duck legs for this recipe.

///////////// //////////////////////////////

Serves 2

1 Preheat the oven to 180ºC/350ºF/gas 4.

2 Place the duck legs in an ovenproof tray and sprinkle with sea salt. Add the cinnamon stick and star anise to the tray and drizzle in the water. Bake for 1 hour and 15 minutes. Remove the duck from the oven, then remove the skin and pick off the meat in strips.

3 To prepare the noodles, boil a full kettle of water, then place the noodles in a heatproof bowl and cover them with the boiling water. Cover the bowl with cling film and allow to sit for 5 minutes.

4 Add the oil to a frying pan over a medium to low heat and fry off the garlic, ginger and duck for 3–4 minutes, until crispy and golden. Add the bok choi and cook for another minute over a medium heat.

5 Uncover the bowl of noodles and drain off the water. Toss the noodles into the pan and add the sweet chilli sauce and soy sauce. Mix, then taste and, if needed, add a small pinch of salt.

6 Serve in some bowls, garnish with the parsley and tuck right in.

2 duck legs, fat trimmed off
sea salt
1 cinnamon stick
2 star anise
100ml water
flat-leaf parsley to garnish

FOR THE NOODLES
250g rice noodles
1 tablespoon olive oil
2 cloves of garlic, chopped
1 teaspoon peeled and grated fresh ginger
1 head of bok choi, sliced into rough pieces
3 tablespoons sweet chilli sauce
2 tablespoons low-salt soy sauce

CHOW MEIN

Chow Mein is a dish of stir-fried noodles. The name originates from the Taishanese chāu-mèing. My take on the dish is simple to prepare but much tastier than anything you'll buy from a Chinese restaurant.

///////////////   ///////////////////////////////////////

Serves 2

1 Put a large pan of water on to boil.

2 Peel and finely slice the ginger and garlic and finely slice the chilli (how much you use depends on how spicy you like things). Slice the chicken into finger-sized strips and lightly season with salt and pepper. Cut the ends off your spring onions and finely slice. Pick the coriander leaves and put to one side, then finely chop the coriander stalks. Halve the bok choi lengthways. If using the mushrooms, either tear into pieces or leave whole.

3 Preheat a wok or large frying pan over a high heat and once it's very, very hot add a good glug of groundnut oil and swirl it around. Add the chicken strips and cook for a couple of minutes, until the meat browns slightly. Add the ginger, garlic, chilli, coriander stalks, mushrooms (if using) and half the spring onions. Stir-fry for 30 seconds, keeping everything moving round the wok quickly.

4 Add your noodles and bok choi to the pan of boiling water and cook for 2–3 minutes – no longer.

5 Meanwhile, add the cornflour, water chestnuts and their water to the wok and give it a good shake to make sure nothing sticks to the bottom. Remove from the heat and stir in 2 tablespoons of soy sauce. Halve the lime, squeeze the juice of one half into the pan and mix well.

1 thumb-sized piece of fresh ginger
2 cloves of garlic
½–1 fresh red chilli
1 large skinless chicken breast
sea salt and freshly ground black pepper
2 spring onions
1 small bunch of fresh coriander
1 bok choi
4 shiitake mushrooms (optional)
groundnut oil
100g medium egg noodles
1 heaped teaspoon cornflour
220g tinned water chestnuts
2–3 tablespoons low-salt soy sauce
1 small lime

6 Drain the noodles and bok choi in a colander over a bowl, reserving a little of the cooking water. Add the noodles and bok choi to the mixture in the wok, adding a little of the cooking water to loosen if necessary, and mix well. Taste and season with more soy sauce if needed.

7 Use tongs to divide everything between two bowls or plates, or to lift onto a large serving platter. Spoon any juices over the top and sprinkle with the rest of the spring onions and the coriander leaves. Serve with lime wedges.

CURRIED CHICKEN SPRING ROLLS

These are an incredible twist on traditional spring rolls. The pineapple salsa with the lime is really refreshing. Make these once and you'll want them again and again.

//////////// //////////////////////////

Serves 4

1 Preheat the oven to 180ºC/350ºF/gas mark 4.

2 Put the chicken onto a baking tray and sprinkle with a pinch of salt and the curry powder, then drizzle with olive oil. Roast in the oven for 20–25 minutes.

3 Dice the red pepper nice and small, and slice the spring onions at an angle. When the chicken is cooked through, cut it into nice small chunks.

4 Add the chicken, spring onion and red pepper to a bowl and drizzle in the sweet chilli sauce. Give it a really good mix with a spoon.

5 To make the salsa, dice up the pineapple really small, finely slice the chives and then zest and juice the lime. Mix all of these together really well in a bowl and set aside until serving.

6 Fill the spring roll wrappers with two heaped tablespoons of the chicken mixture each, then roll the wrapper over the filling, tucking in each side as you do. Double wrap to make sure they don't break while cooking. If you can't get your hands on spring roll wrappers, you can always use filo pastry. Just be careful it doesn't dry out while you are preparing these, so keep it under a damp cloth.

7 Beat the egg and then brush the open edge of the spring roll with it to seal, so the rolls don't open while frying.

2 chicken breasts
sea salt
1 tablespoon curry powder
olive oil
½ red pepper
1 spring onion
4 tablespoons sweet chilli sauce
8 spring roll wrappers
1 egg
olive oil

FOR THE SALSA
½ fresh pineapple
1 bunch of chives
1 lime

8 Fry the rolls over a medium heat in 1–2cm of olive oil for 1 minute on each side until golden and crispy. Once cooked, drain on some kitchen paper.

9 To serve, spoon some of the salsa onto a plate, then slice the rolls at an angle with a serrated knife. Stack two amazing spring rolls on top of the salsa and then serve with a nice bit of salad, micro greens or rocket. These are even better dipped in some extra sweet chilli sauce.

BEEF AND BLACK BEAN SAUCE

I love the salty flavour that black bean sauce has. You can substitute my choices with your favourite veggies in this recipe to make it your own.

//////////// //////////////////////////////

Serves 4

1 Bring a pan of salted water to the boil, add the rice and cook according to the packet instructions. Drain the rice in a sieve, run it under a cold tap to cool, and then allow it to dry out in the fridge.

2 Trim any excess fat from your steak and slice the meat into finger-sized strips. Halve and deseed your pepper and cut it into thin strips. Trim and halve your baby corn lengthways. Peel and finely slice the ginger and garlic. Finely slice the chilli. Cut the ends off your spring onions and finely slice. Pick the coriander leaves and put to one side, and finely chop the coriander stalks.

3 Get yourself a big bowl and in it place the red pepper, baby corn, mangetout, ginger, garlic, chilli, spring onions, coriander stalks and steak strips. Add the sesame oil and mix everything together.

4 Preheat a wok or large frying pan over a high heat and once it's very, very hot add half of the groundnut oil and swirl it around. Add all your chopped ingredients from the bowl. Give the pan a really good shake to mix everything around quickly. Stir-fry for 2 minutes, taking care to keep everything moving so it doesn't burn.

5 Add the black bean sauce, and stir in half the soy sauce and the juice of half the lime. Keep tossing. Taste and season with black pepper.

6 Remove the pan from the heat, transfer everything to a bowl and cover with tinfoil.

130g long-grain or basmati rice
200g sirloin or rump steak
1 red pepper
a handful of baby corn
1 thumb-sized piece of fresh ginger
2 cloves of garlic
½ red chilli
2 spring onions
1 small bunch of fresh coriander
1 handful of mangetout
1 tablespoon sesame oil
1 tablespoon groundnut oil
2 tablespoons good-quality black bean sauce
1 tablespoon soy sauce
1 lime
freshly ground black pepper
1 large free-range egg

7 Give the pan a quick wipe with a ball of kitchen paper and put it back on the heat. Add the rest of the groundnut oil and swirl it around. Crack in your egg and add the remaining soy sauce – the egg will cook very quickly so keep stirring. Once it's scrambled, stir in your chilled rice, scraping the sides and the bottom of the pan as you go. Keep mixing for a few minutes until the rice is steaming hot, then taste and season with a small splash of soy sauce, if needed.

8 Divide the rice between two bowls. Spoon over the meat and black bean sauce and sprinkle over the coriander leaves. Serve with wedges of lime and tuck in!

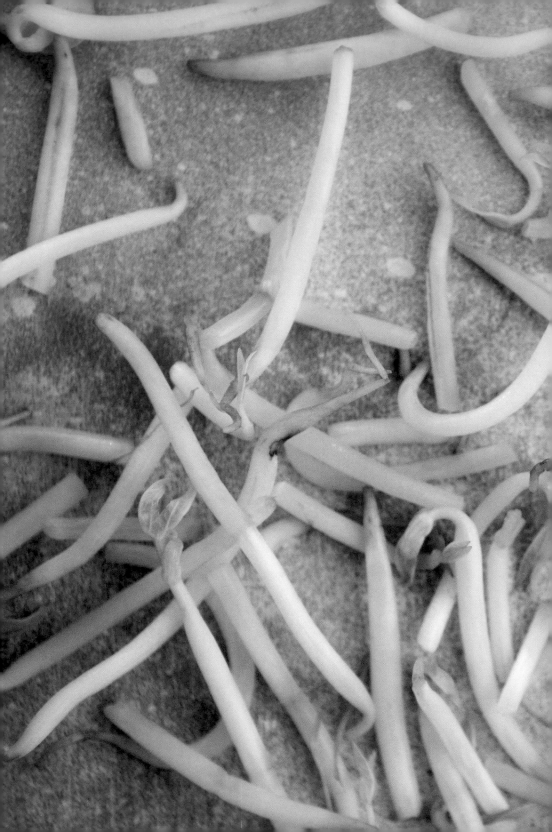

CRISPY DUCK SALAD

You really can't get any better than a salad like this one. If you're feeling lazy you can buy pre-cooked confit duck legs and crisp them under the grill.

////////////// /////////////////////////////////

Serves 4

1 Preheat the oven to 180ºC/350ºF/gas mark 4.

2 Get the duck and pat it dry with kitchen paper, then rub it all over with salt and pepper. Place it in a tray and roast in the oven for around 1 hour 45 minutes, turning it every now and then. Halfway through, you'll probably need to drain away a lot of the fat. Don't throw it away, though! Sieve it and allow it to settle in a bowl. Then use a spoon to separate the fat from the meat juices. The fat can be kept in a jar in the fridge for up to two months and used for roasting potatoes.

3 In a pestle and mortar, bash up the dried chillies and coriander seeds and add a good pinch of salt and pepper. Scoop the seeds out of your squash and put them to one side. Cut the squash into wedges, place them in a roasting tray and drizzle with just enough olive oil to coat. Sprinkle the ground spices over the squash and give it a good toss. Spread the pieces out in one layer.

4 Once the duck has been in the oven for 1 hour, add the tray of squash to the oven and roast for about 45 minutes.

5 Meanwhile, rinse the squash seeds after removing any fibres. Season with salt and pepper and drizzle with olive oil. Toast them in a dry frying pan until they're golden and crisp, and put aside.

6 To make the dressing, put the lime juice and zest into a bowl and add the same amount of extra virgin olive oil, plus the sesame oil and the soy

4 duck legs
sea salt and freshly ground black pepper
1 small bunch of fresh mint, leaves picked and chopped

FOR THE ROAST SQUASH
1–2 dried red chillies, crumbled
1 tablespoon coriander seeds
sea salt and freshly ground black pepper
1 large butternut squash, quartered
olive oil

FOR THE DRESSING
zest and juice of 2 limes
extra virgin olive oil
1 teaspoon sesame oil
1 tablespoon soy sauce
1 fresh red chilli, deseeded and finely chopped
1 clove of garlic, peeled and finely grated
5 spring onions
1 large bunch of fresh coriander, leaves picked and stalks finely chopped

sauce. Stir in the chilli and garlic. Trim the spring onions and finely slice. Add the green spring onion ends and coriander stalks to the dressing. Taste and adjust the sweet-and-sourness by adding more lime juice if needed and then check the seasoning. You want it to be a little limey, to contrast with the rich duck.

7 Once the duck is nice and crispy, and the squash soft and sticky, take both out of the oven. If they need more time, leave them in until perfectly done. Using two forks, shred the duck meat off the bone and put into a large bowl. While the duck and squash are still warm, toss with the toasted squash seeds, half the coriander leaves, half the mint and half the white spring onion slices. Pour on the dressing and toss together. Serve sprinkled with the rest of the coriander, mint and white spring onion slices.

PORK STIR-FRY

A stir-fry is the ultimate fast food. If I'm really stuck for time I'll always turn to a stir-fry. The combo of acidic rice wine and salty dark soy sauce seasons the pork in an amazing way.

/////////////// ///////////////////////////////////////

Serves 4

1 Place one tablespoon of rice wine and one tablespoon of soy sauce in a shallow dish and add the cornflour and sesame oil. Stir in the pork and set aside for 5 minutes.

2 Heat a wok until smoking hot. Add one tablespoon of the sunflower oil. Tip in the pork and stir-fry for 3–4 minutes, until sealed and lightly golden. Transfer to a plate.

3 Meanwhile, place the remaining tablespoon of rice wine and of soy sauce in a small pan with the stock and bring to a simmer.

4 Add the remaining tablespoon of sunflower oil to the wok. Add the ginger and stir-fry for 10 seconds. Tip in the vegetables and continue to stir-fry for 2–3 minutes, until heated through and any leaves are just beginning to wilt, splashing over a little water occasionally to help the greens cook.

5 Return the pork to the wok, then stir in the hot stock mixture. Cook for a minute or so until bubbling, stirring all the time.

6 Spoon the steamed rice into warmed large bowls and spoon the ginger pork and greens on top. Scatter with the sesame seeds and chilli before serving.

2 tablespoons rice wine
2 tablespoons dark soy sauce
2 teaspoons cornflour
1 teaspoon sesame oil
450g pork stir-fry strips
2 tablespoons sunflower oil
120ml chicken stock
5cm piece of root ginger, peeled and finely grated
275g sliced mixed peppers, sliced red onion and bok choi
sticky coconut rice (see page 190)
a handful of sesame seeds
1 long red chilli, sliced thinly

CRISPY HONEY CHILLI CHICKEN BITES

Another Chinese takeaway favourite. Sweet, spicy and absolutely delicious. Try to use good quality local honey as it is a good source of antioxidants. You can bake the chicken in the oven if you don't fancy wok frying it.

/////////// ////////////////////////////

Serves 2

1 Cut the chicken breasts into thin strips. Mix some salt, black pepper and the plain flour in a bowl and coat the chicken with this mixture. Set aside.

2 Peel and finely slice the ginger and cut the chilli into thin strips, removing the seeds.

3 Heat the oil in a wok over a high heat. Meanwhile, juice the lemon into a cup or bowl, add the sweet chilli sauce, soy sauce, water and cornflour and stir together. Leave to one side.

4 Fry the chicken in batches for a few minutes in the hot oil until golden brown, then remove and drain on kitchen paper. Repeat until all the chicken is looking ace!

5 Discard all but about a tablespoon of the oil from the wok, then gently fry the ginger and chilli for a minute or so. Add the honey and stir whilst it is bubbling away for another minute. Then add the lemon juice mixture. Keep stirring and bring to the boil, the sauce will thicken in about 1 minute.

6 Return the chicken to the wok to heat through for a few minutes, tossing in the sauce to coat well. Slice the spring onions into fancy diagonals and throw into the wok for the last minute of cooking.

7 Serve with some naan bread (see page 192) or rice.

2 large chicken breasts
sea salt and freshly ground
  black pepper
200g plain flour
1 thumb-sized piece of
  ginger
1 large red chilli (or more for
  extra heat)
300ml rapeseed oil
1 large lemon
1 tablespoon sweet chilli
  sauce
2 teaspoons soy sauce
80ml water
2 teaspoons cornflour
2 tablespoons honey
a handful of spring onions

WORLD CUISINE

PORK TACOS

Tacos are a traditional Mexican food consisting of a meat or vegetarian filling in a corn or wheat tortilla shell. This is my favourite version, which is made with crispy pork belly. For convenience you can ask your butcher to slice up the pork belly for you.

///////////////   //

Serves 2

1 Mix the red onion, a pinch of sea salt and white wine vinegar together. Leave to sit until serving.

2 To make the tacos, mix the flour, water and salt in a bowl with a fork. Dust a work surface with a little extra flour and knead the dough until smooth.

3 Divide the dough into eight pieces and roll out with a rolling pin until they are half the depth of a one euro coin. Fry them over a medium heat in a dry pan until cooked on either side. You'll know they are cooked once you have a nice golden colour on each side. Allow them to cool down curled around a rolling pin, wooden spoon, or even placed into small bowls just to hold their shape.

4 To prepare the pork belly, put the olive oil in a frying pan over a low to medium heat and add the meat. Sprinkle in the smoked paprika and two good pinches of sea salt and cook until golden and crispy. The pork belly will release a lot of fat and oil, so once it is cooked, remove it from the pan and drain on lots of kitchen paper. Cooking the pork on a low to medium heat will allow most of the fat to render out.

5 Build up the tacos by placing some of the crispy pork into each tortilla. Spoon in some of the red onion and a dollop of yoghurt. Scatter with some fresh coriander, serve with some lime slices and get stuck in.

1 red onion, thinly sliced
sea salt
3 tablespoons white wine vinegar
400g pork belly, sliced
2 tablespoons olive oil
1 heaped teaspoon smoked paprika
2 tablespoons natural yoghurt
1 small bunch of coriander, chopped
1 lime, sliced thinly

FOR THE TACOS
100g wholemeal flour
60g water
a pinch of salt

DONER
KEBAB

I was first introduced to the doner kebab by a chef I worked with in Dublin. He ate nothing but takeaway food! For me, it was like love at first bite, but I knew it couldn't be good for you. Here's one that tastes the same but will not make you feel nearly as guilty.

///////////////// ///

Serves 4

1 Preheat the oven to 180ºC/350ºF/gas mark 4.

2 Place the lamb mince in a large bowl and add the cumin, ground coriander, garlic powder, breadcrumbs and diced onion.

3 Mix all of this with clean hands until well combined. Line an empty 600g tin (for example a bean tin) with heatproof cling film. Pack the mince mixture into this, squashing it in. Place the tin in a deep baking tray filled with water, then put it in the oven to bake for 15–20 minutes. Alternatively you can cook the lamb in a bread tin lined with heatproof cling film, using the same process of filling a tray full of water and baking it in the oven.

4 Once the meat is cooked, stick it with either a metal or wooden skewer and remove it from the tin (it should hold its shape). Slice off pieces of the meat for your kebab. Heat some oil in a frying pan and place the slices of meat into it to colour and get crispy.

5 Make the mayo by combining all the ingredients in a bowl and mixing well.

6 To make up your kebab, place some of the lamb into a pitta bread and then build it like a burger with sweet chilli sauce, some red onion and lettuce, and a dollop of garlic and chive mayo. Find yourself a corner and tuck in. You can also serve this in naan bread by folding over the naan like a taco to hold in the filling.

450g lamb mince
1 teaspoon cumin
1 teaspoon ground coriander
½ teaspoon garlic powder
100g breadcrumbs
1 onion, diced
olive oil

FOR THE GARLIC AND CHIVE MAYO
4 tablespoons mayonnaise
chopped chives
½ teaspoon of garlic powder
 or 2 cloves of garlic, finely
 chopped

TO SERVE
4 pitta breads
sweet chilli sauce
1 head of little gem lettuce,
 sliced

SHISH KEBAB

If you're cooking for a load of friends, or for a party, these kebabs will do the trick. They are easy to make and are damn tasty. Marinated in a blend of spices, they can be grilled, chargrilled or cooked on the 'barbie'.

////////////// //////////////////////////////

Serves 4

1 For the marinade, bash up all the spices in a pestle and mortar until finely ground, then mix with the olive oil to make a thick paste. Put the lamb pieces into a bowl and cover with the marinade. Let them sit there for half an hour to an hour.

2 Then, using the rosemary sticks or skewers, spike each piece of meat alternately with red onion and peppers. Grill on a high heat for around 5 minutes, turning regularly, to give you nicely charred meat on the outside with juicy pink on the inside. Allow to rest for a few minutes before serving – that is, if you can stop yourself from eating them straight away!

500g lamb rump, trimmed and cut into 2½cm cubes
6–8 skewers or sticks of fresh rosemary, lower leaves removed, tips kept on
2 red onions, peeled and quartered
2 red peppers, deseeded and cut into 2½cm pieces

FOR THE MARINADE
1 tablespoon smoked paprika
2 cloves of garlic
½ teaspoon cumin seeds
2 teaspoons coriander seeds
1 tablespoon sea salt
1 teaspoon freshly ground black pepper
100ml olive oil

JERK CHICKEN

Jerk is a style of cooking native to Jamaica in which meat is dry-rubbed or wet marinated with a very hot spice mixture called Jamaican jerk spice. I am obsessed with the spice mixture flavour and how it coats the chicken to make it incredibly crispy and charred.

////////////// //////////////////////////////

Serves 4

1 Pound the allspice berries, peppercorns and chilli flakes in a pestle and mortar until finely ground, then mix in the sugar and honey.

2 Finely chop the parsley, chillies, garlic and ginger, add to the spice mixture and bash it all up some more. Add the green parts of the spring onions and a good drizzle of oil and mix well.

3 Pour the marinade over the chicken and massage it into the meat. Leave to marinate in the fridge for as long as possible, but preferably overnight.

4 Preheat the oven to 200ºC/400ºF/gas mark 6, then cook the chicken for 25–30 minutes, turning occasionally. Finish these off on the barbecue for 5 minutes to get all lovely and charred, or alternatively you can just finish them in the oven.

5 When the chicken is ready, squeeze a little lime juice over it, then take it off the grill or out of the oven and be ready to tuck in. Serve with some crispy sweet potato curly fries (see page 198) and a nice salad.

1 tablespoon allspice berries
1 tablespoon black peppercorns
1 tablespoon dried chilli flakes
½ tablespoon muscovado sugar
2 tablespoons runny honey
a few sprigs of fresh flat-leaf parsley
2 scotch bonnet chillies
1 clove of garlic
3cm piece of fresh ginger, peeled
2 spring onions, trimmed and finely sliced
olive oil
4 chicken thighs, skin on
4 chicken drumsticks, skin on
1 lime

POUTINE

Poutine is a Canadian dish, originating in the province of Québec, made with French fries and cheese curds topped with a light brown gravy. I make mine with a strong cheddar like Dubliner Vintage, as getting cheese curds in Ireland isn't easy.

/////////// ////////////////////////////////

Serves 2

1 Preheat the oven to 200ºC/400ºF/gas mark 6.

2 Combine the potatoes, two tablespoons of oil and a good pinch of salt and pepper in a large bowl, and toss to coat the potatoes.

3 Spread the chips evenly on a large baking sheet and roast in the oven, stirring once or twice, for 20–25 minutes, until the potatoes are tender and browned.

4 Whisk 115ml of beef stock and the flour in a small bowl, then set aside.

5 Heat the remaining three tablespoons of oil in a medium saucepan over a medium heat. Add the mushrooms and onion and cook, stirring often, for 5–7 minutes, until beginning to brown. Add the remaining beef stock and bring to a simmer. Cook for 8–10 minutes, until reduced by about half.

6 Add the reserved flour and stock mixture and continue to cook, stirring constantly, until the gravy is smooth and thickened. Stir in the chives and season with sea salt and pepper. Set the gravy aside and keep warm until needed.

7 When the potatoes are done, push them together in the centre of the baking sheet and sprinkle with the cheese. Return to the oven and bake for approximately 5 minutes more, until the cheese is melted.

8 Serve the potatoes topped with the gravy.

700g new or baby potatoes, scrubbed and cut into quarters
5 tablespoons extra virgin olive oil
sea salt and freshly ground black pepper
350ml beef stock
3 tablespoons plain flour
300g button mushrooms, finely chopped
½ onion, finely chopped
2 tablespoons chives, finely chopped
200g strong cheddar cheese, grated (or cheese curds)

SCALLOPS WITH BLACK PUDDING

Scallops are the ultimate street food in Japan. They normally blowtorch the scallop in the shell and you eat from it with your hands on the go. The addition of black pudding gives this dish the ultimate Irish twist. I consider scallops the sweets of the sea. I highly recommend buying them fresh from a fishmonger, as the frozen ones are rubbery and just not the same. You have to be quick with them, so be well prepared. Make sure you remove the coral from your scallops.

/////////////// ///////////////////////////////////

Serves 2

1 First make the salad. Peel, core and cut the apple into julienne strips. Mix with the lamb's lettuce and season with salt and pepper. Add the zest of almost half the lemon (keeping a little back to garnish) and squeeze over the juice of half the lemon. Drizzle the salad with olive oil and mix well.

2 Heat a large non-stick frying pan over a high heat until smoking hot, then add one tablespoon of olive oil.

3 Lay the scallops out on a board, pat dry with kitchen paper and season one side with salt and pepper. Think of the frying pan as a clock face and add the scallops, one by one, seasoned side down, in a clockwise order, then fry for 1–2 minutes until golden brown. Place the black pudding in the centre of the pan and fry along with the scallops.

4 Season the unseasoned side of the scallops, then flip them over in the same order you placed them in the pan and continue to fry for another 1–2 minutes. Squeeze the juice of the other half of the lemon over the scallops and give the pan a good shake.

1 sharp apple (e.g. Granny Smith)
2 handfuls of lamb's lettuce
sea salt and freshly ground black pepper
1 lemon
olive oil
6 large scallops, cleaned
6 slices of your favourite black pudding

5 When the scallops are cooked, tip the contents of the pan onto a plate lined with kitchen paper. This will instantly stop the cooking process, while the kitchen paper will absorb any excess oil.

6 Divide the salad evenly between two plates, piling it in the middle. Then arrange the scallops and black pudding around each pile. Garnish with a little lemon zest and serve immediately. Alternatively you can go back to this dish's roots and serve it in the shell, just as they do in Japan.

NACHOS

Nachos are the ultimate party food – easy to load and pimp up however you like, and perfect if you've got a group of friends coming round. Traditional nachos consist of fried corn tortillas covered with cheddar cheese and sliced jalapeño peppers, and I haven't strayed far from that, but I do use wholemeal tortillas in mine.

////////////// //////////////////////////////////

Serves 4

1 Cut the tortillas into triangular shapes with a sharp knife. Place the triangles into a pot filled with 1–2cm of hot rapeseed oil and fry them for 1–2 minutes or until crispy. Drain the tortillas on some kitchen paper to remove the oil.

2 Preheat the oven to 180ºC/350ºF/gas mark 4.

3 Place the crispy tortillas onto a baking tray lined with parchment paper. Sprinkle the smoked paprika, cheese, red chilli and sea salt to taste over the tortillas. Bake in the oven for about 5 minutes, just until the cheese is melting.

4 To make the guacamole, blend the avocados, zest and juice of the lime, the coriander and the crème fraîche in a food processor or pestle and mortar.

5 When the nachos are ready to serve, garnish with some extra coriander leaves and lime wedges, and serve with the guacamole on the side, in a bowl for dipping.

8 wholemeal tortillas
rapeseed oil
1 teaspoon smoked paprika
100g cheddar, grated
1 red chilli, thinly sliced
sea salt

FOR THE GUACAMOLE
2 avocados, peeled and
  destoned
1 lime
a handful of coriander
1 tablespoon crème fraîche

SMOKEHOUSE RIBS

Although we don't have great weather for barbecuing in Ireland, these are lovely cooked on the barbecue over a low heat.

//////////// ///////////////////////////

Serves 2

1 Preheat the oven to 150ºC/300ºF/gas mark 2.

2 Mix all the ingredients for the marinade in a bowl.

3 Cut up the ribs into portions and place in an ovenproof dish. Season with salt, then rub in the marinade, sprinkle with the thyme leaves and pour in 200ml of water.

4 Cover with tinfoil and cook for 2 hours. For the last 20 minutes remove the tinfoil and allow to caramelise and get sticky.

5 Serve up with my slaw recipe (see page 196) for the ultimate sticky feast, and enjoy.

600g beef ribs
sea salt
3 thyme sprigs

FOR THE MARINADE
4 tablespoons sweet chilli sauce
4 tablespoons soy sauce
1 tablespoon balsamic vinegar
1 tablespoon honey
2 thyme sprigs
100ml water

CHILLI CON CARNE

Chilli con carne, or chilli as it's known, is an easy one to start with if you are only learning to cook. It also works great as a quick mid-week meal and as a next day, reheated, leftover lunch.

////////////// //////////////////////////////////

Serves 4

1 Dice the onion and finely chop the chilli.

2 Heat some oil in a frying pan over a medium heat, then sweat the onion and chilli until soft. Turn up the heat, add in the mince and cook until golden brown and the fat is evaporated off. The fat will evaporate out through steam on a really high heat.

3 Add in the smoked paprika and cook for 20 seconds, then add the tomato passata, tomato purée, balsamic vinegar and honey. Finish off with the sweet chilli and Sriracha sauces for some heat.

4 Bring the chilli to the boil, then reduce to a simmer, cooking until it has thickened. This normally takes about 10 minutes. Add the kidney beans for the last 3 minutes.

5 While the chilli is simmering, boil your rice – cook for 8–10 minutes with a good pinch of salt.

6 Serve with optional grated cheese and some salad and, of course, enjoy.

1 onion
1 red chilli
olive oil
450g beef mince
1 teaspoon smoked paprika
300g tomato passata
2 tablespoons tomato purée
2 tablespoons balsamic vinegar
2 tablespoons honey
4 tablespoons sweet chilli sauce
2 tablespoons Sriracha sauce
½ x 400g tin of kidney beans, drained and washed
500g brown rice

STICKY WINGS

Sticky, sweet chicken wings are always a winner. This recipe is one I normally cook when the lads are over to watch the football.

////////////// //////////////////////////////

Serves 4

1 Preheat the oven to 200°C/400°F/gas mark 6.

2 Scatter the chicken wings on a roasting tray, season with some sea salt and drizzle with the oil. Roast for 30 minutes.

3 In the meantime make the sauce. In a saucepan on a medium to high heat, sweat the onion and garlic in a little oil until soft, then add the brown sugar and stir until you achieve a dark caramel. This usually takes 30 seconds to 1 minute on a high heat.

4 Once the sugar has caramelised, add in the smoked paprika, ketchup, Worcestershire sauce and sweet chilli sauce and heat through for 30 seconds.

5 When the chicken is cooked, spoon half the sauce over the wings and place them back into the oven for another 5–10 minutes to crisp up.

6 Once crisped up, serve them in a big bowl with the rest of the sauce spooned over and sprinkled with the sesame seeds.

24 chicken wings
sea salt
3 tablespoons olive oil
2 handfuls of sesame seeds

FOR THE SAUCE
½ onion, finely diced
1 clove of garlic, finely chopped
olive oil
1 heaped tablespoon brown sugar
1 tablespoon smoked paprika
4 tablespoons tomato ketchup
1 tablespoon Worcestershire sauce
3 tablespoons sweet chilli sauce

BUFFALO CHICKEN WINGS WITH A SMOKED GARLIC AND CHIVE DIP

A classic wing from the United States. It is normally deep fried and coated in a vinegary, buttery, spicy sauce, but for a healthier version I bake these in the oven. This version has the addition of bourbon to the sauce, which adds an incredible musty flavour. Don't worry, the alcohol burns off in the cooking.

///////////// ///////////////////////////

Serves 4

1 First make the garlic and chive dip. Slice the chives thinly and finely chop or crush the garlic. Mix the chives and garlic into the mayonnaise in a small bowl and set aside until needed.

2 Preheat the oven to 200ºC/400ºF/gas mark 6.

3 Season the chicken wings with the salt and thyme leaves. Now sprinkle the wings with the oil. Give them a good mix with clean hands and place on a baking tray. Roast for 25 minutes.

4 While the wings are cooking, make the sauce. Place the whole bottle of hot sauce in a wide saucepan. Add the white wine vinegar, bourbon and butter and then allow to simmer until the sauce becomes sticky and reduces to a nice syrup consistency.

5 After 25 minutes remove the wings from the oven and dunk them into the sauce. Return them to the oven for another 5 minutes and then dunk them again to get them extra sticky. Place them into the oven for a further 5 minutes and then they are ready. Spoon them into a dish, place the dip on one side, sprinkle with the sesame seeds, chilli and spring onions and tuck in.

24 chicken wings
2 pinches of sea salt
5 sprigs of fresh thyme
3 tablespoons olive oil
1 bottle (354 ml) of hot
   sauce (I prefer Frank's)
100ml white wine vinegar
100ml bourbon
100g butter
a handful of sesame seeds
1 red chilli, sliced
4 spring onions, sliced

FOR THE GARLIC AND CHIVE DIP
4–5 chives
2 cloves of smoked garlic
3 tablespoons mayonnaise

OVEN-FRIED CHICKEN

Growing up, KFC chicken was always a favourite of ours after the cinema or after a good football match. However, it always left you with greasy hands and I always had the feeling that it encouraged spots to break out on my face. So here's my healthier take on it.

///////////// ///////////////////////////////

Serves 4

1 Preheat the oven to 180ºC/350ºF/gas mark 4.

2 Cut the chicken legs through the centre with a sharp knife, separating them into thighs and drumsticks.

3 Sprinkle the chilli powder, garlic powder and salt over the chicken from a height, then drizzle a good glug of oil over the chicken and get your hands in there to mix this all together.

4 Bake the chicken on a tray in the oven for 30 minutes.

5 Set up a station of three bowls on your work surface. Bowl one holds the flour, bowl two holds the beaten egg and milk combined, and bowl three has the wholemeal breadcrumbs mixed with the Cajun spice and a dash of olive oil.

6 After the chicken is cooked, coat it in the mixture by first dipping in the flour, then the egg wash and finally the breadcrumbs. Do it in batches of 2–3 pieces. Try to keep one hand dry and one hand wet. (you'll understand when making it).

7 Put the chicken back into the oven to cook for another 10 minutes.

8 Place the corn on the cob onto a dry pan and char all over for 4–5 minutes, turning every now and again to get an even char and make sure the corn is cooked on all sides.

9 Now serve up the chicken and corn with some slaw (see page 196). I also love these with some garlic mayonnaise, but I'll leave the choice of dip up to you.

6 chicken legs
2 teaspoons chilli powder
1 teaspoon garlic powder
2 pinches of sea salt
olive oil
200g plain flour
2 eggs, beaten
a dash of milk
300g wholemeal breadcrumbs
1 tablespoon Cajun spice
4 small corn on the cob

CAULIFLOWER STEAK

I know this sounds a bit mad, but the flavour is incredible. Try it once – you'll be hooked.

/////////// //////////////////////////

Serves 4

1   Preheat the oven to 180ºC/350ºF/gas mark 4.

2   Firstly prepare the cauliflower. Keeping it whole, with a sharp knife cut off one edge to make it flat. Now cut 2cm in. Repeat cutting the whole way across until you are left with 3–4 steaks (this really depends on the size of the cauliflower).

3   Season the cauliflower with sea salt. Add a glug of oil to a really hot ovenproof pan, then seal the cauliflower steaks on both sides for 2–3 minutes until golden.

4   Add the butter to the pan and allow it to melt. Add the water, then place the pan into the oven for 10–15 minutes until the cauliflower has softened. You can check if its cooked with the tip of a knife or a fork. Serve with some fried rice for the ultimate vegetarian meal.

1 cauliflower trimmed
sea salt
olive oil
2 tablespoons butter
200ml water

PULLED PORK

Pulled pork has become such a trendy street food. While shoulder does take long, slow cooking, it's so worth it, as the result is amazing.

/////////////// //////////////////////////////

Serves 8

1 Mix all the ingredients for the marinade in a pestle and mortar until you have a smooth mixture, crushing the ingredients together.

2 Place the pork in a large, deep pan, add the marinade and turn the pork until coated. Cover and allow to marinate for a couple of hours, or overnight if you have the time. If you don't have the time, don't worry, just get cooking.

3 Place the pan over a high heat, add just enough water to cover the meat (about one litre) and bring to the boil. The water and marinade will combine during cooking to make a wonderful sauce. Reduce the heat, cover with a lid and cook at a steady simmer for 2–2½ hours, until the meat pulls apart easily with a fork. Make sure to turn the pork during the cooking time every 30 minutes.

4 Remove the pork from the sauce with a carving fork and shred, then place the shredded meat on a plate, cover with foil and set aside.

5 Bring the sauce to a steady simmer and reduce for 10–15 minutes, until it is thick (you can sieve the sauce if you like it smooth). Spoon the sauce over the pork and serve in toasted burger buns with some green salad, a little red onion and smoked cheddar. This goes really well with my slaw (see page 196).

1 boneless pork shoulder or neck (about 1.2kg)
8 floury wholemeal baps
1 red onion, sliced
8 slices of smoked cheddar
green salad to garnish

FOR THE MARINADE
140ml Worcestershire sauce
1 tablespoon smoked paprika
120ml ketchup
50g honey
1 medium onion, chopped
2 tablespoons Dijon mustard
2 tablespoons white wine vinegar
½ tablespoon Tabasco sauce
2 tablespoons garlic paste

SOUPS AND SUBS

SLOPPY JOES

This dish originated in the United States during the early twentieth century. Growing up I always recognised Sloppy Joes as the lunchtime meal that kids had in school on TV shows.

///////////////   //////////////////////////////////////

Serves 4

1 Heat a glug of olive oil in a saucepan over a high heat and sweat the onion and pancetta until the meat is crispy. Add the mince and cook until it is golden and all the fat has evaporated out of the mince so it is left dry and crispy. This normally takes about 10–15 minutes.

2 Finely chop the two cloves of garlic and add them to the meat. Then add the chilli powder, tomato purée, Worcestershire and Tabasco sauces and tomato passata.

3 Simmer over a medium heat for 10 15 minutes, then add the sweet chilli sauce and two good pinches of sea salt and cook for a further 5 minutes.

4 Rub or brush the buns with olive oil and toast in the oven until golden and crispy.

5 Now build these bad boys. Slap on about three-quarters of a tablespoon of meat mixture, coat it with loads of grated Parmesan and put on the lid. These are called Sloppy Joes for a reason, so do be prepared with loads of napkins and make sure it isn't your first date! Serve with some steamed greens tossed in butter and salt. I also love these with sweet potato fries (see page 183).

olive oil
1 onion, diced
100g pancetta
450g beef mince
2 cloves of garlic
2 teaspoons chilli powder
2 tablespoons tomato purée
2 tablespoons Worcestershire sauce
2 teaspoons Tabasco sauce
250ml tomato passata
3 tablespoons sweet chilli sauce
sea salt
wholegrain buns for serving
Parmesan, grated

CAJUN CHICKEN MELT

This is a favourite of mine at lunchtime. However, a word of warning: when making this be careful you don't mix up your Cajun spice with blackened Cajun. Blackened Cajun has a serious kick to it that you'd soon know all about.

///////////// ///////////////////////////////

Serves 2

1 To start, place a frying pan on a medium heat. Sprinkle the chicken breasts with the Cajun spice and a little sea salt and drizzle with some olive oil. Then flatten the chicken breasts between two pieces of parchment paper with your hand or a rolling pin.

2 Place the chicken onto the pan and cook evenly on both sides, turning really regularly to evenly colour the chicken. This should take around 8–10 minutes. Once the chicken is cooked slice it up and keep until you are building the melts.

3 While the chicken is cooking you can make the pesto, garlic butter and chilli mayo. For the pesto, crush two cloves of garlic with the pine nuts, two pinches of sea salt and the basil leaves in a pestle and mortar until a paste is formed. Then drizzle in five tablespoons of olive oil and the lemon juice. Mix in the pestle and mortar until well combined and set aside until needed.

4 For the garlic butter, chop up the chives, crush two cloves of garlic and mix these into the room temperature butter.

5 To make the chilli mayo, simply mix the mayonnaise and sweet chilli sauce together.

6 When all the elements are ready, get ready to build these amazing melts. First slice the bread and on each piece spread some of the garlic

2 chicken breasts
2 teaspoons Cajun spice
sea salt
olive oil
4 cloves of garlic
2 tablespoons pine nuts
2 handfuls of basil leaves
juice of ½ lemon
3–4 chives
100g butter, at room temperature
4 tablespoons mayonnaise
1 tablespoon sweet chilli sauce
bread of your choice (I like ciabatta)
300g Vintage Dubliner cheese

butter. On top of this place the sliced chicken and then spoon a dollop of chilli mayo on top.

7 Now let's totally pimp this recipe. Grate the cheese over the melt (and remember you can never have enough cheese) and drizzle with pesto. Finally bake in a preheated oven at 190ºC/375ºF/ gas mark 5 or grill on medium for 6–8 minutes. Then just tuck in.

THE **CHICKEN** FILLET **ROLL**

Every deli counter in Ireland sells a chicken fillet roll. Students live on them for lunch. Here's my healthy version. It may take a little longer to make your own, but at least you know exactly what has gone into it.

Serves 4

1 First, make the rolls. In a large bowl mix all the dry ingredients together. Then, using a fork, mix in the water. Once a dough forms, place it onto a flour-dusted surface and knead for 5–10 minutes until smooth and soft. Place the dough back into the bowl and cover with a damp tea towel in a warm area until it doubles in size.

2 Once the dough is ready, preheat the oven to 180ºC/350ºF/gas mark 4.

3 Cut the dough into four pieces and roll into a nice bread roll shape. Place the rolls onto a tray lined with parchment paper and score the top of each three to four times with a knife. Brush the rolls with a little beaten egg and sprinkle with chia seeds. Bake for 25 minutes.

4 Put some flour in a bowl and dust each chicken breast, then dip them into the beaten egg. In another bowl mix together the Cajun spice and wholemeal breadcrumbs, and dip the chicken into the breadcrumb mix. Place the chicken on a baking tray, sprinkle with sea salt and drizzle with oil, and bake for about 25 minutes at 180ºC/350ºF/gas mark 4. The timing really depends on the size of the chicken breasts you use – just make sure there isn't a sign of pink meat when you cut it. You can bake the rolls and chicken together to save time.

5 Now it's time to assemble them. Slice your rolls in half and slice the chicken in strips. Layer some mayonnaise onto your rolls, then add the chicken and some rocket leaves, and you're ready to go.

FOR THE CHIA ROLLS
500g wholemeal flour
a pinch of caster sugar
a pinch of sea salt
1 x 7g sachet of fast action yeast
325ml water
1 egg, beaten
chia seeds

FOR THE CHICKEN
plain flour for dusting
4 chicken breasts
3 eggs, beaten
2 tablespoons Cajun spice
wholemeal breadcrumbs
sea salt
olive oil
mayonnaise
rocket leaves (optional)

MEATBALL SUB

This takes me back to living off Subway in college. All I ever wanted for lunch was a meatball sub. I used to think it was somewhat healthy, but then realised that we were all being fooled. So here is a proper meatball sub that is much better for you than anything you will buy. I usually make a big batch of the meatballs and freeze them, coated in sauce. Then I pop them straight into the oven covered with tinfoil to reheat.

///////////// ///////////////////////////////

Serves 6

1 Preheat the oven to 220ºC/425ºF/gas mark 7.

2 Cut away and discard the crusts on the stale bread, then tear into chunks and place in a bowl. Cover with cold water and leave to soak.

3 Finely slice the sausages, two cloves of garlic and the parsley leaves, then place into a large bowl with the mince, eggs and Parmesan. Squeeze the water out of the bread and add to the bowl.

4 Using your hands, scrunch and mix everything together, seasoning well with salt and pepper, then divide and roll into twelve equal-sized balls. Place in a roasting tray (about 25cm x 30cm), drizzle with a little olive oil and put in the fridge for about 10 minutes to firm up.

5 Meanwhile, finely chop the remaining garlic cloves, the onion and chilli. Drain and finely chop the peppers.

6 Place the meatballs into the hot oven for 15–20 minutes, or until golden, shaking the tray from time to time to stop them from sticking, then place directly over a low heat on the hob. Add the wine, allow it to boil and bubble away, then stir in the onion, garlic and chilli and cook for

100g stale bread
80g quality sausage
4 cloves of garlic, peeled
½ bunch of fresh flat-leaf
  parsley, leaves picked
400g quality beef mince
400g quality pork mince
2 large free-range eggs
30g Parmesan, grated
sea salt and freshly ground
  black pepper
olive oil
1 onion
½ fresh red chilli, deseeded
1 x 450g jar of roasted red
  peppers
50ml white wine
2 x 400g tins of plum
  tomatoes
balsamic vinegar
150g mozzarella
6 soft wholemeal bread rolls

a few minutes, or until turning golden. Stir in the peppers and the plum tomatoes, breaking them up with the back of a spoon, then season and add a splash of balsamic vinegar.

7 Return the tray to the hot oven for 20–30 minutes, or until the meatballs are cooked through. Remove from the oven. Cut the mozzarella into twelve slices, then carefully place one slice on top of each meatball and return the meatballs to the oven for a further minute, or until the cheese has melted.

8 Open out the bread rolls, fill each with two cheesy meatballs, spoon over the tomato sauce, then add another drizzle of balsamic vinegar. Push down on the sandwich to squidge it shut and enjoy.

ROAST BEEF SUB WITH GRAVY

I've had this on the go in London several times. I'm always on the lookout for a good food market that does a quality roast beef and gravy sub in Ireland, but have yet to find one. Maybe that's a business idea for someone.

/////////////// ///////////////////////////////////

Serves 6

1 Take your beef out of the fridge 1 hour before it goes into the oven and allow to come to room temperature.

2 Preheat your oven to 200ºC/400ºF/gas mark 6.

3 There's no need to peel the vegetables – just give them a wash and roughly chop them. Break the garlic bulb into cloves, leaving them unpeeled.

4 Add 3 tablespoons of oil to a large frying pan over a medium heat and sweat off all your vegetables for a minute to release the flavour. Remove them from the pan and place into a roasting tray.

5 Season the beef well with sea salt and cracked black pepper.

6 Using the same frying pan, seal the beef all around, making sure to get a nice even golden colour. Place the beef carefully on top of the vegetables in the roasting tray, add the rosemary and thyme on top and place in the oven. Cook for 1 hour for medium beef or leave for another 15–20 minutes for well done.

7 Baste the beef halfway through cooking and if the vegetables look dry, add a splash of water to the tray to stop them burning. When the beef is cooked to your liking, remove it to a warmed dish, cover with some tinfoil and allow to rest.

1½kg quality rib of beef
1 onion
½ leek
1 bulb of garlic
4 tablespoons of whatever oil you have in the cupboard
Sea salt and cracked black pepper
2 sprigs of rosemary
2 sprigs of thyme
4 shallots, cut in half and peeled
6 wholemeal rolls
some rocket leaves

FOR THE GRAVY
juices from the beef
300ml beef stock
1 sprig of rosemary, kept whole
2 tablespoons Worcestershire sauce
cornflour for thickening

8 While the meat is resting make your gravy. Remove the vegetables from the juice in the roasting tray, then add the beef stock, rosemary and Worcestershire sauce to the juice. Allow it to boil up, then thicken with some cornflour.

9 Slice the beef thinly with a sharp knife. Put the sliced beef into the gravy and simmer on a low heat for 5 minutes.

10 In the meantime, add a tablespoon of oil to a frying pan over a high heat and fry the shallots on each side until golden and caramelised.

11 Slice your rolls and then toast them. Now assemble. Put some roast beef and gravy on the lower part of the roll, add some shallots and rocket leaves and cover with the top of the roll. You can even add some grated cheese if you like.

CHICKEN
BONE BROTH

If you've visited New York recently you'll have noticed this new fast food trend. Broth shops are opening everywhere and specialise in these bone broths. Once you have it made you can pimp it up with different vegetables, such as bok choi, sautéed mushrooms, spring onions and chillies. You can also use this in gravy or as stock.

///////////// /////////////////////////////////

Serves 6

1   Preheat the oven to 200ºC/400ºF/gas mark 6, then roast your chicken bones for 25–30 minutes.

2   Once the bones are ready, place all the ingredients into a really large saucepan. Simmer for 6–10 hours (the longer the better), skimming the fat occasionally.

3   Remove from the heat and allow to cool slightly. Strain the liquid through a colander into a bowl, discarding the solids. Let the broth cool slightly and tuck in, adding chopped vegetables and noodles to make this a filling soup (I like rice noodles, bean sprouts and bok choi).

4   Use within a week, or freeze for up to 3 months.

1.75kg chicken bones
3 carrots, chopped
3 celery stalks, chopped
2 medium onions, unpeeled, sliced in half lengthwise and quartered
4 cloves of garlic, unpeeled and smashed
1 teaspoon Himalayan salt
1 teaspoon whole peppercorns
2 tablespoons apple cider vinegar
2 bay leaves
3 sprigs fresh thyme
5–6 sprigs parsley
1 teaspoon oregano
18–20 cups cold water (enough to fill the saucepan)

BEEF BONE BROTH

Broths are fantastic for sports people who are suffering from injuries. Beef bone broth is one of the most healing foods you can consume. It's rich in nutrients like gelatin and glycine, which help to protect and heal your leaky gut, skin, digestive tract, muscles, etc.

As with the chicken version, you can also use this in gravy or as stock.

Serves 6

1   Preheat the oven to 200ºC/400ºF/gas mark 6, then roast your beef bones for 25–30 minutes.

2   Once the bones are ready, place all the ingredients in a really large saucepan. Bring to a boil over a high heat, then reduce the heat and simmer gently, skimming the fat that rises to the surface occasionally. Simmer on a very low heat for 24–48 hours to extract all the goodness from the bones. I know it sounds like a long time but trust me it's worth it. If you are time poor, 6 hours will do on a medium to high heat.

3   Remove from the heat and allow to cool slightly. Strain the liquid through a colander into a bowl, discarding the solids. Let the broth cool slightly and tuck in, adding chopped vegetables and noodles to make this a filling soup (I like rice noodles, bean sprouts and bok choi).

4   Use within a week, or freeze for up to 3 months.

- 1.75kg beef bones with marrow
- 4 carrots, chopped
- 4 celery stalks, chopped
- 2 medium onions, unpeeled, sliced in half lengthwise and quartered
- 4 cloves of garlic, unpeeled and smashed
- 1 teaspoon sea salt
- 2 tablespoons apple cider vinegar
- 1 teaspoon whole peppercorns
- 2 bay leaves
- 3 sprigs of fresh thyme
- 5–6 sprigs of parsley
- 18–20 cups cold water (enough to fill the saucepan)
- 1 tablespoon tomato purée

VEGETABLE SOUP

This soup just warms you up when it's cold. I love the barley in it as it adds an amazing texture. This is a great dish for the car. Just put it into a travel mug and away you go. Street food at its best.

/////////// ///////////////////////////////

Serves 6

1 Place the pearl barley in a sieve and rinse well under cold running water.

2 Heat the oil in a pan over a medium heat and add the celery, onion, carrot, leek and thyme. Sauté for 15 minutes, until the vegetables are softened.

3 Pour in the stock, then add in the rinsed barley and bring to the boil. Reduce the heat and simmer for about 20 minutes or until the vegetables and barley are completely tender.

4 Now stir in the parsley and season to taste with sea salt and pepper. Serve with some nice brown bread.

50g pearl barley
1 tablespoon olive oil
2 celery sticks, diced
1 onion, diced
1 carrot, diced
1 small leek, trimmed and diced
1 tablespoon chopped fresh thyme
1.2 litres vegetable stock or chicken stock (use a low or no salt stock cube)
1 tablespoon chopped fresh flat-leaf parsley
sea salt and freshly ground black pepper

TIP: It's a great idea to make up larger quantities of this soup and freeze the extra portions. Make sure to label and date the food so you know when it was made. It will last for up to two months in your freezer.

THAI GREEN CURRY

The green colour comes from the green chillies in this recipe. The first time I made it, I added spinach purée to the curry and it ended up going luminous green. So don't make the same mistake.

///////////// //////////////////////////////////

Serves 4

1   First make the curry paste. Peel and roughly chop the garlic, shallots and ginger and place in a food processor.

2   Trim the lemon grass, remove the tough outer leaves, then finely chop and add to the processor. Trim the chillies and add along with the cumin and the coriander (stalks and all). Blitz until finely chopped, then add the fish sauce and blitz again.

3   Slice the chicken into 2½cm strips. Heat one tablespoon of oil in a large pan on a medium heat, add the chicken and fry for 5–7 minutes, or until just turning golden, then remove the pan from the heat and transfer the chicken to a plate.

4   Tear the mushrooms into even pieces. Return the pan to the heat, add the mushrooms and fry for 4–5 minutes, or until golden. Transfer to a plate using a slotted spoon.

5   Reduce the heat slightly and add the curry paste. Cook for 4–5 minutes, stirring occasionally, then pour in the coconut milk and boiling water, crumble in the stock cube and add the lime leaves. Turn the heat up and bring gently to the boil, then simmer for 10 minutes, or until reduced slightly.

6   Stir in the chicken and mushrooms, reduce the heat to low and cook for a further 5 minutes, or until the chicken is cooked through, adding the mangetout for the final 2 minutes.

7   Season to taste with sea salt and freshly ground black pepper. Pick, roughly chop and stir through the basil and coriander leaves. Serve with lime wedges and steamed rice.

750g skinless free-range
  chicken thighs
groundnut oil
400g mixed mushrooms
1 x 400g tin of light coconut
  milk
400ml boiling water
1 organic chicken stock cube
6 Kaffir lime leaves
200g whole mangetout
sea salt and freshly ground
  black pepper
½ bunch of fresh basil
¼ bunch of fresh coriander
1 lime

FOR THE CURRY PASTE
4 cloves of garlic
2 shallots
5cm piece of ginger
2 lemon grass stalks
4 green bird's eye chillies
1 teaspoon ground cumin
¼ bunch of fresh coriander
2 tablespoons fish sauce

CURRIED MEATBALLS

This is an amazing twist on classic Italian meatballs and works so well with the spices.

//////////// /////////////////////////////////

Serves 4

1 Preheat the oven to 220ºC/425ºF/gas mark 7.

2 Place all the ingredients for the meat mix excluding the oil into a bowl and mix really well with a wooden spoon. Shape into twelve small balls approximately 2.5cms in diameter. Put the meatballs in a large roasting tin, drizzle with camelina oil and bake in the oven for 7 minutes.

3 Meanwhile make the sauce. Place a saucepan or frying pan with some oil over a medium heat and sweat down the onion for 30 seconds, then add the curry powder and tomato purée and cook for another 30 seconds. Add the coconut milk, ginger, soy sauce and salt and bring to the boil.

4 Take the meatballs out of the oven, pour the sauce over them and place back into the oven for another 7 minutes.

5 Rinse the rice under cold water to wash off the dust and starch, then place it into a pot with a lid, along with the cardamom, water and salt, and bring to the boil rapidly. Turn down the heat and allow to simmer for 8–10 minutes until light and fluffy. Remember to remove the cardamom pods once cooked – they should be sitting at the top of the rice when it is ready.

6 For the garnish, in a hot frying pan coated with some oil, flatten little pancakes of grated potato and fry on a medium heat until golden and crispy on each side.

7 When everything is ready, serve on a decorative platter by spooning on the rice, then the meatballs, sauce and garnish, and tuck in.

FOR THE MEAT MIX
300g beef mince
300g pork mince
1 egg, lightly beaten
1 spring onion, finely sliced
a small piece of ginger, grated (about a teaspoon's worth)
½ teaspoon cumin
a pinch of sea salt
camelina oil

FOR THE SAUCE
olive oil for frying
½ onion, sliced
1 tablespoon mild curry powder
2 tablespoons tomato purée
1 x 400ml tin of coconut milk
a small piece of ginger, grated (about a teaspoon's worth)
1 tablespoon soy sauce
a pinch of sea salt

FOR THE RICE
300g basmati rice
3 cardamom pods, pierced to release the flavour
600ml water
2 big pinches of sea salt

TO GARNISH (OPTIONAL)
olive oil
1 Maris Piper potato, peeled, grated and any water squeezed out

BEEF SATAY

Satay is a delicious peanut sauce which can be served with any meat you like. You can use chunky peanut butter if you like a crunchy texture.

/////////////// ///////////////////////////////////

Serves 4

1   Remove the steak from the fridge 30 minutes before cooking and allow to come to room temperature.

2   Sweat the onion, garlic and lemon grass in some oil in a saucepan over a low heat for a minute until soft. Add the curry powder and peanut butter and stir through for another minute. Add the soy sauce and coconut milk, then turn up the heat and bring to the boil. Simmer on a low heat until ready to serve and season to taste with sea salt if needed. Add the dry roasted peanuts, if using, for a nice crunch.

3   Once you have the sauce made, cook the steak. Heat some oil in a large pan and season the steak with sea salt and cracked black pepper. First, seal the steak for 2 minutes on each side on a really high heat, then turn down the heat and cook for a further 2 minutes on each side. Remove from the pan – at this stage your steak should be medium/medium rare.

4   Slice the steak up and add it to the satay sauce. Allow to cook for a further 5 minutes in the sauce on a medium heat. Serve in a bowl with some fluffy rice and enjoy.

400g sirloin steak
½ onion, diced
2 cloves of garlic, crushed
¼ stick of lemon grass,
  bashed and chopped finely
olive oil
2 tablespoons mild curry
  powder
3 heaped tablespoons
  peanut butter
1 tablespoon soy sauce
1 x 400g tin of coconut milk
sea salt
2 handfuls of dry roasted
  peanuts (optional)
cracked black pepper

PRAWN
PAD THAI

This isn't your authentic Pad Thai recipe, but it's a simple twist on it that tastes very similar and uses easily accessible ingredients that we have here in Ireland. You can always substitute your favourite meats like chicken or beef if you don't like prawns. Most supermarkets now stock smoked garlic and baby spring onions. But if it happens that they don't, just use the ordinary varieties, giving the spring onions a small chop.

///////////// ///////////////////////////////

Serves 2

1   Place the noodles in salted boiling water and cover for 5 minutes to soften.

2   Chop the garlic, coriander stalks, lemon grass and chilli, then fry in some oil for a minute over a medium heat. Add the prawns and spring onions and cook for another 2–3 minutes.

3   Add the lime zest and juice and the bean sprouts. Now add the noodles to the pan and stir well until heated through. Season with sea salt to taste and serve sprinkled with the chopped peanuts and coriander leaves.

200g rice noodles
2 cloves of smoked garlic
a handful of coriander, leaves and stalks separated
¼ stick of lemon grass
1 red chilli
olive oil
10 Dublin bay prawns shelled and de-veined (ask your fishmonger)
10 baby spring onions
zest and juice of 2 limes
100g bean sprouts
sea salt
a handful of salted peanuts, chopped

MASSAMAN CURRY

My first time eating massaman curry was on a successful date. So for that reason I highly recommend it. Its flavour is really distinctive and it normally has delicious sliced potatoes served in it.

///////////// ///////////////////////////////////////

Serves 4

1   First season the chicken with some sea salt, then cook it on a high heat for 5 minutes on each side. Take it off the pan and slice it into bite-sized pieces. The chicken will still be raw in the centre at this stage but don't worry, it's meant to be.

2   Heat the oil in a saucepan over a medium heat, then add the onion, garlic and ginger and sweat for 2 minutes.

3   Reduce the heat, then add all the spices and a teaspoon of salt and cook for 1–2 minutes.

4   Add the coconut milk, about 200ml of water and the potatoes and turn the heat up to high. Cook for 10–15 minutes without a lid so the sauce reduces. Now add the chicken and simmer on a medium to high heat for 5 minutes.

5   Finish the curry by adding in the peanuts and stirring through as much coriander as you like.

6   Now serve it all up with your favourite rice dish and enjoy! I love this with the cauliflower rice on page 190.

4 chicken breasts
sea salt
1 tablespoon olive oil
1 onion, chopped
2 cloves of garlic, chopped
1 teaspoon chopped fresh ginger
1 teaspoon Chinese five spice
1 teaspoon ground cumin
¼ teaspoon cayenne pepper
¼ teaspoon turmeric
1 x 600g tin of coconut milk
3 large Maris Piper potatoes cut into ½-inch pieces
½ cup chopped peanuts
1 bunch of chopped coriander

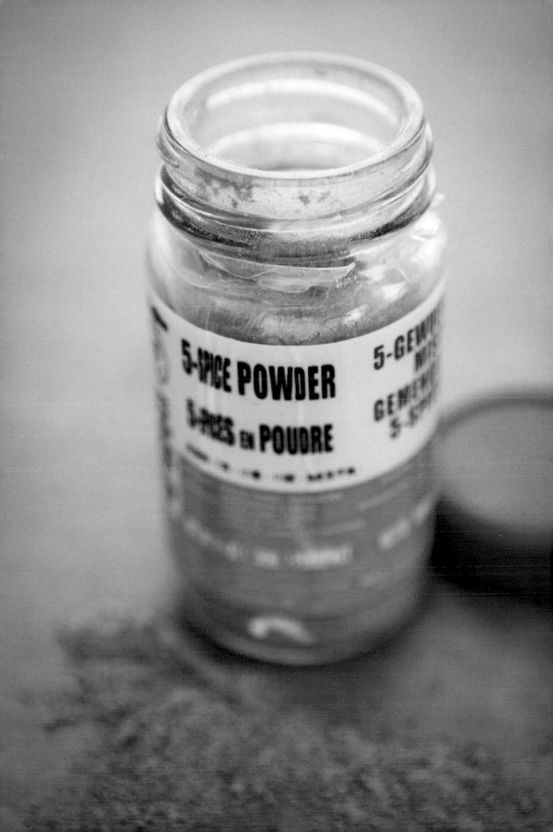

FISH CAKES

A fish cake is normally breaded but these ones are a bit different. I love the addition of fish sauce. It smells horrible, I know, but added to certain dishes gives an incredible flavour.

//////////////// /////////////////////////////////////

Serves 4

1   Put the whiting, beans and basil in the food processor and whizz until just combined – you don't want it too smooth. Remove to a bowl, add the fish sauce, curry paste, lemon zest and a pinch of black pepper. Mix well, then add in the beaten egg. Shape into eight fish cakes 2–3cm thick.

2   Heat the oil in a large frying pan and add in half the fish cakes. Fry gently until golden and cooked through, making sure to turn them to get both sides golden. This will take about 10 minutes. Cover with tinfoil and keep warm while you cook the remaining fish cakes.

3   Meanwhile make up the sauce by putting the rice wine vinegar, sugar, chilli, salt and garlic in a saucepan. Chop up the coriander stalks and add them to the saucepan. Keep the leaves to use later.

4   Heat gently until the sugar melts.

5   Combine the water and cornflour and stir it into the mixture. Gently simmer until the sauce thickens. Set aside to cool, then add in the cucumber and the chopped coriander leaves.

6   To serve, drizzle the sauce over the fish cakes. These go really well with my mojito courgetti (see page 199).

700g whiting, skinned, boned and diced
120g green beans, trimmed
a handful of basil leaves
2 tablespoons fish sauce
2 tablespoons red curry paste
zest of 1 lemon
freshly ground black pepper
1 egg, lightly beaten
1 tablespoon sunflower oil

FOR THE CHILLI AND CORIANDER SAUCE
120ml rice wine vinegar
40g brown sugar
1 red chilli
2 pinches of sea salt
2 cloves of garlic
1 handful of fresh coriander
60ml water
1 teaspoon cornflour
a small piece of cucumber (4–5cm), chopped

WESTERN EUROPE

A CHEEKY NANDO'S

This one feeds my obsession with the restaurant Nando's. I have an obsession with piri-piri chicken, to the extent that when I visited Portugal it's all I ate! You'll need the pestle and mortar twice for this recipe.

///////////////   ///////////////////////////////

Serves 4

1 Let's start with the chicken. If you have a good sharp knife then you can do this yourself, but don't be afraid to ask your butcher if you'd rather. Split the chicken right down the middle, so it's cut in half. You'll be left with a leg, wing and breast on each side. With your knife trim off any bits of fat and bone that are left hanging.

2 Once this is done, make the marinade by bashing together the thyme, sea salt and smoked paprika in the pestle and mortar. Drizzle in the red wine vinegar and stir. Spoon this marinade over the chicken and massage it in with your hands. Allow to marinate overnight if you can.

3 Heat a griddle pan until smoking hot and char the skin of the chicken until it is golden and crispy. This normally takes about 4 minutes on a hot pan.

4 Place the chicken onto a baking tray and bake for 40 minutes at 180ºC/350ºF/gas mark 4 or until it is fully cooked. (Cooking time will depend on the size of your chicken.)

5 While the chicken is cooking, make the salsa. Cut the tops off the chillies and add them to the pestle and mortar. Add the coriander, lemon zest and sea salt, and muddle it into a paste. Add the juice of the lemon, along with the olive oil, and mix.

6 Once cooked, slice the chicken, place it onto a board and spoon over the salsa. This dish is especially good with sweet potato fries and slaw (see pages 183 and 196).

1 x 1kg chicken

FOR THE MARINADE
8 sprigs of thyme
a pinch of sea salt
1 teaspoon smoked paprika
2 tablespoons red wine vinegar

FOR THE SALSA
2 whole green chillies
a handful of coriander
zest and juice of 1 lemon
a pinch of sea salt
2 tablespoons olive oil

STEAK BURRITO

Burrito places are popping up everywhere. With this recipe you can always change the meat and filling to your liking. Make sure to buy the best meat you can afford.

////////////// /////////////////////////////////

Serves 2

1 Season the steak with salt and pepper on both sides. Pour some oil onto a smoking hot pan, then add the steak. Cook the meat for 2 minutes on both sides on the high heat, then turn down the heat and cook to your liking.

2 While the steak is cooking, slice your red onion, lettuce and cherry tomatoes to whatever size you like. Make a curry mayonnaise by mixing the mayonnaise with the curry powder. Grate the Vintage Dubliner and set aside until assembly.

3 Take the steak off the heat, place it onto a plate and set aside to rest. In the pan you cooked the steak in throw in the pre-cooked rice to heat. Add a knob of butter and the lime juice and heat through on a medium heat for 3–5 minutes.

4 To assemble the burritos, lay the wholemeal wraps on a piece of tinfoil. Spread on the curry mayonnaise, then add the tomatoes, lettuce, and red onion.

5 Slice up the steak and add to the wraps, then sprinkle with the Dubliner and spoon over the rice.

6 Fold up the base of the wrap using the tinfoil to help and then tuck in both sides. Grate some Parmesan over the top and allow it to melt to add a finishing touch.

7 Now its time to plate up. Cut each burrito in half, place on a plate and serve with some of the crispy sweet potato fries on page 183. Enjoy.

1 sirloin steak, cut in half
sea salt and cracked black
  pepper
olive oil
1 red onion
½ head of iceberg lettuce
8 cherry tomatoes
3 tablespoons mayonnaise
1 teaspoon mild curry
  powder
200g Vintage Dubliner
  cheese
½ pack of pre-cooked
  wholemeal rice
knob of butter
juice of ½ lime
2 wholemeal wraps
a small piece of Parmesan

GINGER BEER BATTERED FISH

I first tried this when feeding the staff in a restaurant where I was allowed to go wild and experiment with different recipes. The ginger beer gives a subtle flavour and an incredible lightness to the batter, so I can confidently say that the experiment was a complete success. Ask your fishmonger to remove the pin bones from the fish for you, as this can be very fiddly to do.

///////////// ///////////////////////////

Serves 2

1 Preheat the oven to 190ºC/375ºF/gas mark 5.

2 Pour the sunflower oil into a large frying pan and place over a medium to high heat. Mix the salt and pepper together and season the fish fillets on both sides. This will help to remove any excess water, making the fish really meaty.

3 Whisk the flour, ginger beer and baking powder together until nice and shiny. The texture should be like semi-whipped double cream (i.e. it should stick to whatever you're coating). Dust each fish fillet in a little extra flour, then dip into the batter and allow any excess to drip off.

4 Holding one end, carefully lower each piece of fish into the oil one by one so you don't get splashed – it will depend on the size of your fryer how much you can do at once. Cook for 4 minutes or so, until the batter is golden and crisp.

5 Place the fish fillets on a baking tray and put them in the oven for a few minutes to finish cooking.

6 When the fish is done, drain the pieces on kitchen paper, season with some salt and squeeze over a little lemon juice. I love to serve this fish with some Parmesan fries (see page 184).

400ml sunflower oil for shallow-frying
½ teaspoon sea salt + extra for seasoning
1 teaspoon freshly ground black pepper
225g white fish fillets, pin-boned
225g flour + extra for dusting
285ml ginger beer, cold
3 heaped teaspoons baking powder
1 lemon

CHICKEN GOUJONS WITH LEMON MAYONNAISE

My mum found it hard to find something I would eat growing up, as I was extremely fussy. Goujons were one of the things that kept me fed and happy. In my recipe I love the way the sesame seeds add specks through the breadcrumbs. And, of course, they taste good too.

//////////// ////////////////////////////

Serves 4

1 In a bowl mix the flour with two pinches of sea salt. Put the beaten egg in a separate bowl, and in a third bowl or on a plate mix the breadcrumbs with the sesame seeds and curry powder.

2 Toss the chicken in the seasoned flour mixture, then dip each piece in the beaten egg and then in the breadcrumbs.

3 Heat the oil in a wok or wide saucepan over a medium heat and shallow fry the chicken for 8–10 minutes until it is nice and crispy. Remove and drain on some kitchen paper. As an alternative, you can cook the chicken in an air fryer at 180ºC/350ºF for 25–30 minutes until cooked through (this timing will depend on your air fryer).

4 Mix the mayonnaise and lemon zest and juice in a bowl really well. You could also add your favourite herbs, chopped up, to the mayonnaise.

5 Serve up the goujons and mayonnaise together, along with my sweet potato fries of course (see page 183).

3 tablespoons plain flour
sea salt
2 large eggs, beaten with a drop of milk
80g fine fresh wholemeal breadcrumbs
2 handfuls of sesame seeds
1 tablespoon mild curry powder
4 medium-sized chicken breasts, each cut into 3 pieces
5 tablespoons olive oil
6 tablespoons mayonnaise
zest and juice of ½ lemon

THE SPICE BAG

The latest trendy thing to eat across Ireland is the spice bag. It's sold in Chinese takeaways, but was invented in Ireland. With this dish, it's all about the spice mixture. Here's my version.

/////////////// ///////////////////////////////////

Serves 2

1 Preheat the oven to 200ºC/400ºF/gas mark 6.

2 To make the chips, slice the potatoes to whatever thickness you like. Sprinkle with the chopped rosemary and sliced onion, coat with the coconut oil and bake for 35–40 minutes. Make sure you mix all the ingredients with your hands before cooking. If your tray isn't non-stick, use some greaseproof or parchment paper.

3 To prepare the chicken, place the strips into the beaten egg. In a separate bowl mix the cumin and ground almonds, then place the chicken strips into the mixture, ensuring they are fully coated. If you find they aren't fully coated, go back and dip into the egg and then back into the ground almond mix once more.

4 Place the chicken onto a baking tray, put it in the oven and bake for 20–30 minutes.

5 Mix the spices together in a small bowl. Once cooked, combine the chicken and chips and then from a height sprinkle the spice mix over them, making sure to coat both the chicken and chips.

6 I recommend serving this in a bag or wrapped up in some newspaper, with a sprinkling of red and green sliced chilli.

2 chicken breasts, sliced into small strips
2 eggs, beaten
½ teaspoon cumin
200g ground almonds
1 teaspoon coconut oil
sliced red and green chilli (optional)

FOR THE CHIPS
4 medium-sized Maris Piper potatoes, washed
2 sprigs of rosemary, chopped
1 onion, sliced
1 tablespoon coconut oil, melted

FOR THE SPICE
2 good pinches of sea salt
1 tablespoon Chinese five spice
½ teaspoon garlic powder
½ teaspoon chilli powder

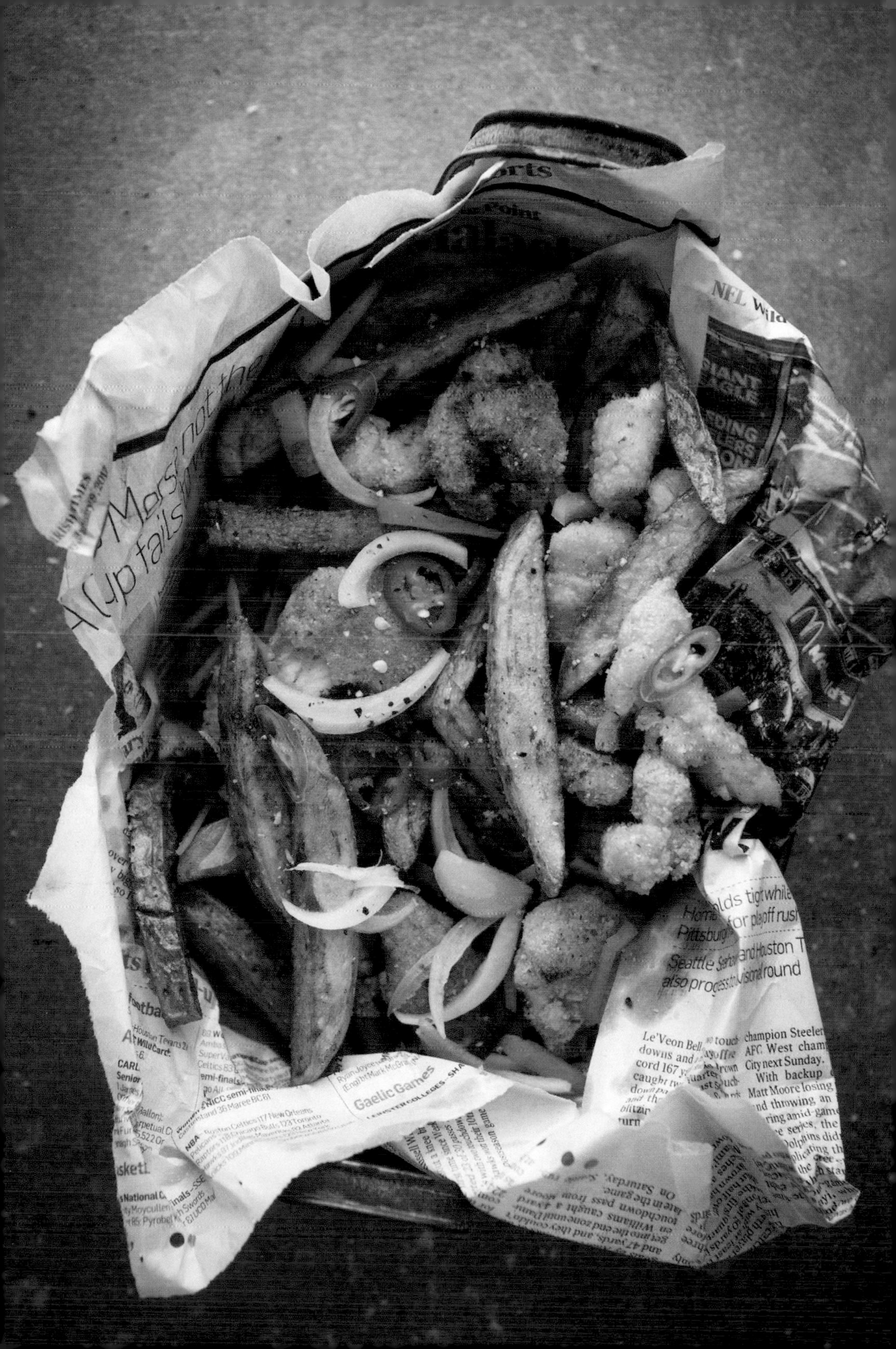
Gaelic Games
With backup
Matt Moore losing

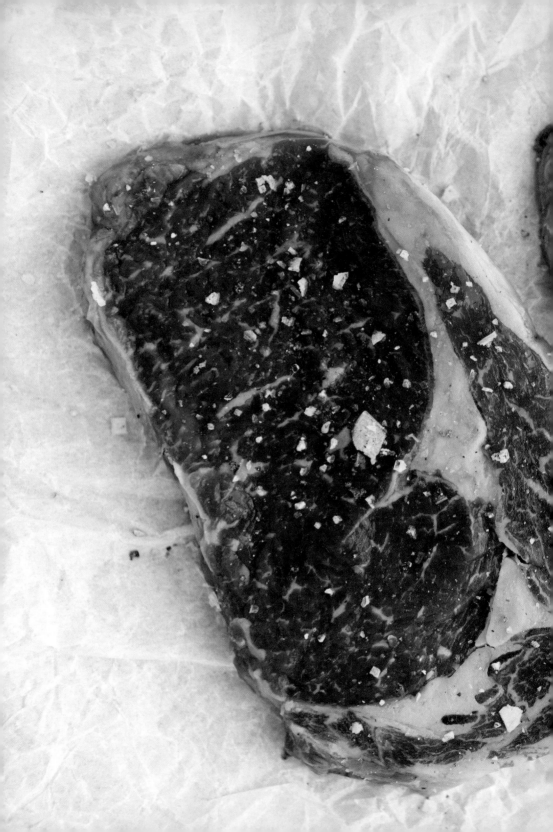

STEAK WITH PEPPER SAUCE

I eat steak at least once a week. I love all the different cuts there are to choose from. I highly recommend going to your butcher for steak, as they can really help you choose the best cuts. The cooking guide provided here works great with sirloin, striploin, fillet, rib-eye, flank and skirt steak. How long you need to cook your steak to achieve your liking really depends on how thick it is. Checking the steak by touch really makes a difference. Knowing the different tensions can really tell you how cooked it is. Soft means it's rare/medium rare, springy means it's medium and solid means well done. Use a spoon or tongs of course, so you don't lose your fingerprint!

FIVE STEPS TO COOKING THE PERFECT STEAK AT HOME

1 Take the steaks out of the fridge 30 minutes before cooking to allow them to come to room temperature.

2 Lightly brush the steak with a little olive oil and season with sea salt and freshly ground black pepper just before cooking.

3 Heat your griddle or frying pan over a high heat, until smoking hot. Don't griddle more than two steaks at a time, and keep them spaced well apart. If you add more than two steaks to the pan at once, the temperature will drop and the steak will stew rather than fry.

4 Seal each side of the steak with some fresh thyme and crushed garlic for 30 seconds on a very high heat, then finish cooking in a preheated oven at 190ºC/375ºF/gas mark 5 to your liking (see timings overleaf).

5 Let the steak rest for about 5 minutes (in tinfoil) before serving, to allow the juices that have been drawn to the surface to relax back into the meat.

FOR THE PEPPER SAUCE (FOR 2 STEAKS)

- 200ml balsamic vinegar (I like using a flavoured balsamic like blackberry)
- 2 sprigs of thyme
- 200ml beef stock
- 300ml cream
- 2 good pinches of cracked black pepper

HOW LONG TO COOK A STEAK FOR

These timings are based on cooking a steak that's about 3cm thick. (Cooking times will vary depending on the type and thickness of the steak, and how hot your pan is.)

Blue: 1 minute each side. No oven required.

Rare: 1½ minutes in the oven (after searing).

Medium rare: 2½ minutes in the oven (after searing).

Medium: 4 minutes in the oven (after searing).

Medium–well done: 5–7 minutes in the oven (after searing).

TO MAKE THE PEPPER SAUCE

Add the balsamic vinegar and thyme to the pan you cooked the steak in, then reduce by half. Add the beef stock and again reduce by half. Stir in the cream and allow to thicken. Finish by stirring in the black pepper. Serve immediately over your steak. Hasselback potatoes go great with a good steak.

SPATCHCOCK CHICKEN (PIRI-PIRI STYLE)

The spatchcock idea actually came from Ireland in the eighteenth century, when we needed to whip up a simple, quick meal. The Portuguese then took our idea, added piri-piri, and Nando's was born. Spatchcocking is a great way of getting a whole roast chicken cooked in a short space of time. The trick is to find yourself a good butcher who can spatchcock your chicken for you. They will do it in seconds.

////////////// //////////////////////////////////

Serves 4

1 To spatchcock the chicken, flip it over so the backbone is facing you. Using a sturdy pair of kitchen scissors or a sharp knife, cut down either side of the backbone, then discard the bone. Turn the chicken over and push down firmly on the breastbone to flatten out the bird. Make a few slashes in each leg joint to help.

2 Put the chillies and garlic in a food processor with a good pinch of salt, or use a pestle and mortar. Blend to a paste, then add the paprika, vinegar, parsley (reserving some to garnish), thyme leaves and olive oil. Mix well, then smear over the chicken. Leave to marinate for at least 1 hour, or overnight if possible. This can be frozen at this stage if you want to have it prepped well in advance.

3 Fire up the barbecue. When the flames have died down, season the chicken with a couple of pinches of sea salt and place it on the centre of the barbecue, skin-side down. Cook for 15–20 minutes until nicely charred. Flip the chicken over and continue cooking for another 5–15 minutes until cooked through. Check that the juices run clear, as the heat of every barbecue varies. (To cook in the oven, preheat to 190ºC/375ºF/gas mark 5 and cook for 40–45 minutes on a baking tray. To char the skin, grill for a further 5–10 minutes.) Serve with lemon wedges, some of the chopped parsley and my stuffed sweet potato skins (see page 200).

1 medium-sized chicken (about 1½kg)
4 red chillies, chopped (deseeded if you don't like it too spicy)
3 cloves of garlic, crushed
sea salt
2 teaspoons sweet paprika
2 tablespoons red wine vinegar
1 good bunch of flat leaf parsley, finely chopped
3–4 sprigs of thyme, leaves removed
2 tablespoons olive oil
1 lemon

STUFFING, GRAVY AND CHIPS

This one sounds a bit odd but tastes amazing. It is served in chippers up where I am from, on the border of Fermanagh and Cavan. Traditionally served with ordinary chips, the sweet potato version makes this super healthy.

/////////////// ///////////////////////////////

Serves 2

1 Preheat the oven to 200ºC/400ºF/gas mark 6.

2 Make the gravy. Trim and roughly chop the celery and carrots, then peel and quarter the onions. Finely chop the bacon. Put the vegetables and the herbs into a sturdy, high-sided roasting tray and scatter the bacon on top.

3 Break the chicken wings open, then put them onto a board and bash the bones up; this will release more of their flavour. Put them in the pan, drizzle with oil, sprinkle over a few pinches of sea salt and black pepper, then toss everything together and put the tray in the oven to cook for 1 hour, or until the meat is tender and falling off the bone.

4 Take the pan out of the oven and put it on a hob over a low heat. Use a potato masher to really grind and mash everything up. Keep mashing, moving and scraping all the goodness from the bottom of the pan as you go. Gradually mix in the flour to thicken the mixture – the longer you let everything fry, the darker your gravy will be.

5 When the flour is combined pour in the white wine and two litres of hot water, turn the heat up and bring to the boil for 10 minutes until thickened, then turn down the heat and simmer for about 25 minutes, stirring occasionally.

6 Turn the oven temperature down to 180ºC/350ºF/gas mark 4.

2 sweet potatoes, washed
  and cut into wedges
2 teaspoons cumin
1 teaspoon cayenne pepper
1 teaspoon smoked paprika
sea salt and freshly ground
  black pepper
3 sprigs of rosemary,
  roughly chopped
olive oil
a handful of semolina

FOR THE STUFFING
check stuffing recipe (see
  page 201)

FOR THE GRAVY
2 sticks of celery
2 carrots
2 onions
2 rashers of smoked streaky
  bacon
2 fresh bay leaves
2 sprigs of fresh rosemary
8 chicken wings
olive oil
sea salt and freshly ground
  black pepper
4 tablespoons plain flour
60ml white wine (optional)

7 Cut the sweet potatoes into nice sized chips. I like mine chunky but if you like them skinny, then go nuts.

8 Spread the chips out on a large baking tray and sprinkle with the spices, a good pinch of salt and pepper and the rosemary. Drizzle with enough oil to coat them, then mix really well with your hands.

9 Sprinkle the chips with the semolina flour from a height. Bake for 35–45 minutes depending on the size you cut them. Keep an eye on them and give them a shake every 10 minutes. (Alternatively you can air fry these chips which gives them an incredible crunch.)

10 Make your stuffing (see page 201).

11 When the gravy has reached the consistency you're looking for, check the seasoning then push it through a sieve into a large bowl – really push and mash everything through so you get as much flavour as possible. Discard anything left behind.

12 Now to assemble. In a nice bowl scatter in the sweet potatoes. Spoon over some stuffing and then finish with the gravy. You're sure to enjoy this one.

PATATAS BRAVAS

When people go out for tapas, Patatas Bravas is the side dish that most of them go for. You can also get this on the go in certain areas in Spain. If you are making these for visitors, you can make the sauce well in advance, keep it in the fridge and simply reheat it just before the potatoes are ready to serve.

//////////////   ////////////////////////////////

Serves 4

1 Preheat the oven to 200ºC/400ºF/gas mark 6.

2 Cut the potatoes into small cubes and pat dry with kitchen paper. Spread over a roasting tin and toss in 2 tablespoons of the oil, then season. Roast for 40–50 minutes, until the potatoes are crisp and golden.

3 About 15 minutes before the potatoes are cooked, heat the remaining oil on a high heat in a pan, add the onion and fry for about 5 minutes until softened. Add the garlic, tomatoes, tomato purée, paprika, chilli powder, sugar and a pinch of salt and bring to the boil, stirring. Simmer for 10 minutes until pulpy.

4 Tip the potatoes into dishes and spoon over the sauce. Sprinkle with the parsley and, if you want to be really authentic, serve with cocktail sticks.

900g potatoes
5 tablespoons olive oil
sea salt and freshly ground
** black pepper**
1 onion, chopped
2 cloves of garlic, chopped
1 x 227g can of chopped
** tomatoes**
1 tablespoon tomato purée
2 teaspoons sweet paprika
a pinch of chilli powder
a pinch of sugar
fresh parsley, chopped

BEEF CARPACCIO

I first tried this in St Tropez in France and went on to learn how it was made when I worked in Bon Appetit. It is traditionally served raw, but I sear the outside of mine to create a crust and flavour on the outside. Even though this dish apparently originated in Venice, it is another great tapas dish. You can mix and match various herbs for the marinade, or just use one.

///////////// /////////////////////////////////

Serves 4

1   Bring a large pot of salted water to the boil. Drop in the beans and cook for about 5 minutes. When perfectly done, drain them in a colander.

2   To make the marinade, mix the chopped shallots in a bowl with the handful of herbs, the mustard, vinegar and extra virgin olive oil. Season with salt and pepper to taste, then add the hot cooked beans and toss. Put to one side to allow the beans to cool down and take on all the fantastic flavours.

3   Place the beef fillet on a chopping board and season it all over with salt and pepper. Run the thyme sprigs under hot water for a few seconds – this will help to release their fragrant oils. Strip the leaves from the stalks and chop them up roughly. Sprinkle the thyme leaves over the fillet, then roll the meat around the chopping board so that any excess seasoning and herbs stick to it.

4   Get a heavy frying pan very hot and add a splash of oil, followed by the beef fillet. Fry for 1 minute only, turning it every few seconds to sear and encrust all the lovely flavourings onto it. Remove the meat from the frying pan and put it onto a plate to rest for a minute. (Once seared, you can serve straight away or you can keep the meat covered on a plate until needed. I prefer not to keep it in the fridge.)

250g green or mixed beans, topped and tailed
2 small shallots, very finely chopped
1 handful of fresh soft herbs (e.g. chervil, parsley, yellow inner celery, tarragon), leaves picked and chopped
1 teaspoon Dijon mustard
1½ tablespoons white wine vinegar
4 tablespoons extra virgin olive oil + extra for drizzling
sea salt and freshly ground black pepper
500g quality beef fillet
a few sprigs of fresh thyme
olive oil for frying

5 Slice the seared fillet with a sharp knife. Lay each slice on a board and flatten as much as you can by pressing down on them with the side of a chopping knife. Lay two or three slices out flat on each plate. Season again lightly and place a pile of beans on top, spooning over some of the marinade. Sprinkle over any leftover herb leaves and drizzle with some good extra virgin olive oil.

THE SAUSAGE ROLL

A true Irish twist on the classic sausage roll. Once you get the hang of the folding, these are very simple to put together. There was some discussion when I mentioned including this, as my editor wasn't convinced this was a fast food – I leave it up to you to decide. You can see a video of how to make these at http://chefadrian.ie/the-clonakilty-sausage-roll.

Serves 4

1 Preheat the oven to 200ºC/400ºF/gas mark 6.

2 Remove the skins from the sausages and place the meat into a bowl. Dice the black and white pudding and then add it to the sausage meat. Give it a really good mix with a spoon and set aside.

3 Cut the pastry into quarters. On each quarter make five equally spaced cuts along both the long edges towards the centre of the pastry, leaving about a centimetre of uncut pastry down the middle. This will give you six flaps of pastry on each side. Fold up the set of flaps at each end of the pastry, forming a rounded end that flanks the uncut middle. Add a quarter of the filling along the middle right to the folded-up ends. Fold the remaining flaps of pastry over the top of the filling. Repeat with the other three pastry squares.

4 Place the sausage rolls onto a tray lined with parchment paper. Crack the egg into a small bowl, whisk with a fork and then brush over the sausage rolls.

5 Top them with sesame seeds and chia seeds and bake for 15 minutes. And you know the drill. Eat, repeat, enjoy!

½ packet (454g) of good quality sausages
100g black pudding
100g white pudding
1 sheet of puff pastry
1 egg
a handful of sesame seeds
a handful of chia seeds

LA SOCCA

In all my travels to France, this fast food really stood out for me. I had this in Nice, a town that has its own 'Niçoise' cuisine, which is really different. I had La Socca in the main food market, where they have this small cart to bring it to and from a pizza oven in a local restaurant. Its crispy texture and flavour are really distinct. Chickpea flour can usually be found in organic food shops. Why not try serving it as a tapas or a snack?

///////////////// ///////////////////////////////////

Serves 4

1 Pour the water into a bowl, then sprinkle in the flour like a fine rain while mixing with a whisk.

2 Add the salt and oil. Mix well to make a paste. Let the paste stand for 1 hour to let the gluten rest.

3 Pour the paste onto an oiled pizza pan or a baking tray. The thickness of the paste should not exceed 3mm. You can pour on rounds like pancakes or fill the whole tray with the mixture.

4 Preheat your grill to its maximum temperature for 10 minutes. Place the dish in the middle of the grill and let it cook for 5–7 minutes, keeping an eye on the colour: the Socca should be well toasted but not burnt.

5 Remove the dish from the grill and serve immediately by cutting into portions and sprinkling with freshly ground black pepper.

250ml water
125g chickpea flour
2 pinches of sea salt
2 tablespoons olive oil
Freshly ground black pepper

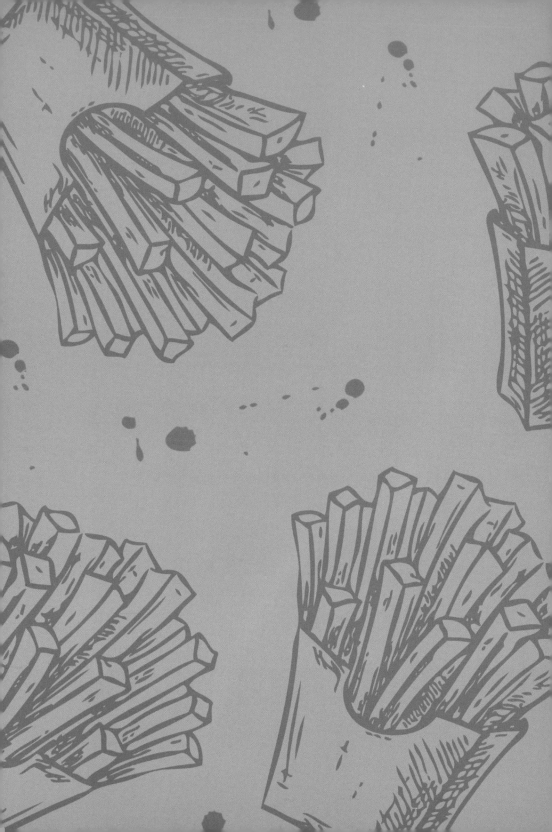

SIDES

FRIED RICE

Fried rice can be eaten on its own as a main meal, or as an accompaniment to other dishes. It is a great way of using up leftover boiled rice. The recipe I have here is for an accompaniment, but by adding meat or prawns could be made into a main meal. If you don't have any leftover rice, simply cook some fresh while you are preparing the vegetables.

//////////////   //////////////////////////////

Serves 2

1 Heat the oil in a large frying pan and stir-fry the garlic, chilli and ginger for 1 minute. Add the spring onions, carrots and red pepper and stir-fry for a further 3 minutes.

2 Stir through the sesame oil, soy sauce and Thai fish sauce and cook for 1 minute. Add the peas and gently mix through, then add the cooked rice to the pan and mix to combine with the vegetables.

3 Make a well in the centre and pour in the whisked egg. Allow to set briefly, then, working quickly, stir the egg and quickly incorporate the rice from the sides until everything is combined. Cook for 2 minutes more, then serve straight away in a big bowl with your favourite main course. I love it with the butter chicken (see page 30).

1 tablespoon olive oil
2 cloves of garlic, peeled and finely grated
1 red chilli, deseeded and finely chopped
1 thumb-sized piece of fresh ginger, peeled and finely grated
4 spring onions, thinly sliced
2 large carrots, peeled and thinly sliced
1 red pepper, deseeded and finely chopped
1 teaspoon sesame oil
1 tablespoon soy sauce
1 tablespoon Thai fish sauce (Nam Pla)
150g frozen peas
300g cooked rice, cold
2 large free-range eggs, lightly whisked

SWEET POTATO FRIES

These can be quite tricky to get crispy. The addition of semolina really coats the sweet potato and gives them a crispy outer layer.

/////////////// ///////////////////////////////

Serves 2

1 Preheat the oven to 180ºC/350ºF/gas mark 4.

2 Cut the sweet potatoes into nice-sized chips. I like mine chunky, but how big you cut them is up to you. Spread them out on a large baking tray and then sprinkle with the spices, a good pinch of salt and pepper, and the rosemary. Drizzle with some oil and mix really well with your hands.

3 Sprinkle the semolina flour over the potatoes from a height. Bake in the oven for 35–45 minutes, depending on the size you cut them. Keep an eye on them and give them a shake every 10 minutes. (Alternatively you can air fry these chips which gives them an incredible crunch.)

4 Serve up as an amazing side dish and enjoy.

2 sweet potatoes, washed
2 teaspoons cumin
1 teaspoon cayenne pepper
1 teaspoon smoked paprika
sea salt and freshly ground
  black pepper
3 sprigs of rosemary roughly
  chopped
olive oil
a handful of semolina flour

PARMESAN
FRIES

This recipe feeds my addiction to Parmesan. The more mature the Parmesan, the better the flavour. I highly recommend buying it in a good artisan food store with a cheese counter for the best quality fries.

///////////// //////////////////////////////////

Serves 2

1 Preheat the oven to 190ºC/375ºF/gas mark 5.

2 Cut the potatoes into skinny fries and place onto a baking tray lined with parchment paper. Drizzle with the oil, sprinkle with the rosemary and sea salt and bake for 35 minutes.

3 Once cooked, remove from the oven and then grate over as much Parmesan as you like (I find it hard to stop).

4 Maris Piper potatoes
olive oil
4 sprigs of thyme
sea salt
Parmesan

SWEET POTATO AND PARMESAN SAMOSAS

The first time I made a samosa was while studying international cuisine in Killybegs catering college. They were tricky to put together at the start but after a lot of practice they can be made really easily. Once you get the hang of them they are the most satisfying dish to make.

//////////// ////////////////////////////

Serves 4

1 Put the sweet potatoes in a large bowl, cover with cling film and microwave on high for 8 minutes or until soft.

2 Meanwhile, heat two tablespoons of oil in a large pan, add the chopped onion and cook for a few minutes to soften. Stir in the ginger, garlic, chilli (if using) and coriander stalks, stirring for a couple of minutes more until fragrant (the garlic will burn easily, so keep an eye on it).

3 Add the curry paste and half the nigella seeds to the pan, stir for 30 seconds or so until fragrant, then add the spinach and two to three tablespoons of cold water. Cook the spinach until wilted, then add the sweet potato and any liquid from the bowl.

4 Season well and mash everything together with the back of a spoon, leaving some chunky bits of potato. Stir in the Parmesan and leave to cool completely.

5 Preheat the oven to 180ºC/350ºF/gas mark 4.

6 Unroll the pastry and pull out two sheets to work with – keep the rest covered with a tea towel to prevent them from drying out. Brush both sheets with a little oil and scatter some of the remaining nigella seeds over one sheet. Put the other sheet on top. With the shortest side facing

2 large sweet potatoes (about 500g), peeled and cut into small pieces
olive oil
2 red onions, 1 chopped, 1 halved and finely sliced
1 thumb-sized piece of ginger, peeled and finely chopped
2 cloves of garlic, crushed
1 fat red chilli, finely chopped (optional)
1 small bunch of coriander, stalks finely chopped, leaves picked
2 tablespoons curry paste (I used Balti)
2 teaspoons nigella seeds
200g spinach (fresh or frozen)
100g Parmesan, grated
270g pack filo pastry (6 sheets)
½ cucumber
150ml natural yoghurt

you, cut down the centre to make two long strips. Scoop a sixth of the sweet potato mixture onto the top right-hand corner of a pastry strip. Fold the pastry over on an angle, continuing down the length of the pastry until you reach the bottom and have a neat triangle encasing the filling. Trim off any excess pastry with a knife. Repeat to make six samosas.

7   Put the samosas on a baking tray lined with baking parchment. Brush with a little more oil and sprinkle over the remaining nigella seeds. Bake for 25–30 minutes or until a deep golden brown.

8   Meanwhile, using a vegetable peeler, cut the cucumber into ribbons, then toss with the sliced onions and coriander leaves. To serve, dollop some yoghurt onto each plate, top with two samosas and a mound of the cucumber salad.

ONION BHAJIS

An absolute must as an accompaniment to curry, or a wonderful starter for an Indian meal.

/////////////// ////////////////////////////////

Serves 4

1 Kick off by slicing the onions nice and thin, then place them in a bowl with the flour.

2 Whisk up the 2 eggs and slowly add them into the flour to make a batter. Add the coriander and cumin to the flour mixture and stir.

3 Taking tablespoon amounts of the mixture, fry it in 2cm of hot oil for about 2 minutes each side.

4 Sprinkle some sea salt over the bhajis when they come out of the oil and place them on a tray lined with kitchen paper.

5 Serve with sweet chilli sauce or as a side to a curry.

3 onions
120g plain flour
2 eggs
1 teaspoon ground coriander
1 teaspoon cumin
200ml vegetable oil
sea salt

STICKY COCONUT RICE

Sticky rice is that delightful concoction that can be found accompanying many Asian dishes, most often Thai or Indonesian main courses. It's also known as sweet or glutinous rice. I love the addition of coconut milk. Make sure you use the full fat though, as it's much thicker and won't split as easily.

/////////////// ///////////////////////////////////////

Serves 2

1 Rinse the rice in several changes of water until the water is no longer cloudy.

2 Add all the ingredients to a small pot and bring to the boil. Cover, reduce the heat to low and allow to steam for 15 minutes.

3 Remove the cover, fluff the rice with a fork and serve immediately.

1 mug of basmati rice
200ml coconut milk
½ mug of water
a pinch of sea salt

CAULIFLOWER RICE

A great low-carb substitute for rice, and I find that it tastes better too.

/////////////// ///////////////////////////////////////

Serves 2

1 Place the cauliflower into a food processor and pulse until it forms small rice-like particles.

2 Heat the oil, butter and garlic in a frying pan over a medium heat, then add the cauliflower.

3 Cook for 4–5 minutes, then stir in the parsley.

4 Serve with your favourite curry or stir-fry as a tasty, low-carb substitute to rice.

1 head of cauliflower,
  separated
2 tablespoons olive oil
2 tablespoons butter
2 cloves of garlic, finely
  chopped
1 bunch of parsley, chopped

HASSELBACK POTATOES

If I were in Italy I'd call her La Nonna. Our whole family – cousins, aunties and uncles – used to come together on a Sunday at her house and she presided over it like an Italian matriarch. These potatoes were one of her specialities, but you'd be very lucky to get one, and with so much competition, you had to be quick. These are a really different alternative chips, and perfect with a steak or burger.

///////////// //////////////////////////////////

Serves 4

1 Preheat the oven to 200ºC/400ºF/gas mark 6.

2 Rest each potato on top of two chopsticks or in the curve of a wooden spoon, and then slice all along the potatoes, leaving about 2mm between the cuts. The purpose of the chopsticks or wooden spoon is to stop you cutting fully through the potatoes.

3 Brush the potatoes with oil, then sprinkle with thyme and sea salt. Place them onto a baking tray with 200ml of water, then roast for about 40 minutes or until crispy and cooked. Before serving grate the Parmesan over them and allow to melt. Enjoy.

6 Maris Piper potatoes, washed with skin on
olive oil
3 sprigs of fresh thyme, leaves removed and chopped
a good pinch of sea salt
200g Parmesan

NAAN BREAD

Naan, nan or khamiri seems to have originated in northern India, but it is now a staple in the cuisines of west, central and southern Asia. My first time making this bread was in culinary college, where each week we got to choose an international cuisine we liked. This is the recipe I cooked when we were cooking Indian. I've tweaked it since then by adding the nigella seeds.

/////////////// ///////////////////////////////////////

Serves 4

1 In a bowl, combine the yeast, honey and lukewarm water, then set aside for 5 minutes, or until starting to bubble.

2 Melt the butter in a small pan over a low heat. Meanwhile, combine the flour and half a tablespoon of salt in a large bowl and make a well in the middle. Pour in one tablespoon of the melted butter, the yoghurt and the yeast mixture, and beat the wet ingredients together with a fork. Gradually start incorporating the flour from the sides until the mixture starts to form a rough dough, then bring it together with your hands – it should be soft and sticky, so add a splash more water if you think it needs it.

3 Knead the dough on a flour-dusted surface for around 5 minutes, or until smooth, then place into a lightly floured bowl. Cover with a clean tea towel and leave in a warm place for 1 hour 30 minutes, or until doubled in size.

4 Once risen, knock back the dough with your fist, then divide into six balls. Roll each portion into an oval shape, roughly 1½cm thick.

5 Heat a large non-stick frying pan over a high heat, add one of the ovals and cook for 5–6 minutes, or until cooked through, turning halfway. Brush with a little of the remaining melted butter. If the butter has gone solid again, just melt it over a low heat. Then sprinkle with a few nigella seeds and a small pinch of salt. Keep warm in the oven while you make the remaining breads. Serve with your favourite curry.

½ x 7g sachet of dried yeast
1 teaspoon runny honey
125ml lukewarm water
45g unsalted butter
250g strong white bread flour + extra for dusting
sea salt
3 heaped tablespoons low-fat natural yoghurt
1 tablespoon nigella seeds

WHITE PUDDING CROQUETTES

This is the ultimate croquette. The white pudding adds an amazing flavour to the mashed potato and the crispy outside is incredible. This is a great side for the roast beef sub with gravy.

///////////// ///////////////////////////////

Serves 4

1 Firstly make the mash by boiling and simmering the potatoes until tender. Give them a good mashing with either a masher or, if you like no lumps, put them through a ricer.

2 Add the butter, cream and salt to the mashed potato and mix until smooth and soft.

3 Dice the white pudding on a board and add to the mashed potato.

4 Allow the mix to cool before shaping the croquettes. Form cylinders out of the mash. When shaping, take your time and dust them with flour so they don't go sticky and fall apart.

5 Once you have the cylinders, crack the eggs into a bowl and then whisk in the milk.

6 Dip the croquettes into the egg and milk mixture and then coat them in breadcrumbs. In a wok filled with 2cm of hot oil, fry until golden and crispy.

7 Serve with your favourite roast dinner or even on their own as a snack for tea.

5 large Kerr's Pink potatoes, peeled and halved
1 tablespoon butter
100ml cream
a pinch of sea salt
200g white pudding
plain flour for dusting
2 eggs
200ml milk
400g breadcrumbs
rapeseed oil for frying

FOCACCIA BREAD

This is my most favourite bread ever. You can make this with different flavours, but my favourite is the combination of thyme, garlic and sea salt flakes I have used here. I first tried it in college in DIT, where each student made their own flavour combo. I fell in love with it right then. It's important when making this one to use a good quality olive oil.

////////////// /////////////////////////////////////

Serves 4

1 First make the dough by combining all the dry ingredients in a mixing bowl. Then pour in the water and mix with a spoon until it comes together. Tip onto a work surface dusted with a bit of flour and knead for 10 minutes until well combined – when you press your finger into the dough it should spring back. Place it back into the mixing bowl and cover with a damp tea towel and allow to prove for an hour in a warm place.

2 After an hour prepare your baking tin by greasing it with a little olive oil. Take the dough and spread it across your baking tin with your finger tips pressing down hard on it to make loads of different grooves.

3 Remove the thyme leaves from the sprigs and drizzle with some oil so they don't burn in the oven. Then press the thyme leaves and garlic into the different grooves in the dough. Once you have your filling placed into the different grooves, sprinkle with two pinches of sea salt.

4 Cover with the damp tea towel again and leave to prove for 20 minutes more. While the bread is proving, preheat the oven to 200ºC/400ºF/gas mark 6.

FOR THE DOUGH
500g of strong flour + extra for dusting
1 x 7g sachet of yeast
pinch of salt
pinch of sugar
325ml tepid water

FOR THE TOPPING
good quality olive oil
8–10 sprigs of fresh thyme
10 cloves of garlic, peeled and halved
3–4 pinches of sea salt

5 Once proved, remove the tea towel and place the bread into the oven for 20 minutes, until crispy on top and fluffy inside.

6 As soon as it's cooked remove from the oven and drizzle well with olive oil to give it an amazing shine and help flavour it. Sprinkle with the rest of the sea salt, remove from the tin and serve.

HEALTHY
SLAW

Slaw has always been the ultimate accompaniment to take-out food. Replacing the mayonnaise with yoghurt really brings down the calories, but we bring back the flavour with the lemon.

/////////////// ///////////////////////////////////

Serves 6

1 This can be made really easy if you have a food processor with a slicing attachment. If you do, just fire the cabbage and onions through the food processor. If you don't have a luxurious blender, then use the coarse side on a box/cheese grater and some elbow grease!

2 Once all that work is done, in a large bowl mix the honey, white wine vinegar, lemon zest and juice, salt and Greek yoghurt.

3 Toss in the onion and cabbage and give it a really good mix using your hands. You can serve this immediately or it will keep, covered with cling film, for 3–4 days in your fridge.

½ red cabbage, grated
2 red onions, grated
3 tablespoons honey
3 tablespoons white wine
  vinegar
zest and juice of ½ lemon
a good pinch of salt
6 tablespoons Greek
  yoghurt

SWEET POTATO CURLY FRIES

This recipe works nicely in the air fryer as it's much healthier this way than deep frying. Heads up – you will also need that trendy spiralizer.

////////////// /////////////////////////////

Serves 2

1 Preheat your air fryer to 160ºC/320ºF.

2 Run the sweet potato through the coarse blade on a spiralizer.

3 In a bowl mix the seasoning, oil and semolina, then add the spiralized sweet potato and mix until the potato spirals are completely coated.

4 Place the spirals into the air fryer to cook, keeping an eye on them until they are crispy and delicious. Mine took 15 minutes, but I find every air fryer to be different.

1 sweet potato, scrubbed
1 teaspoon salt
¼ teaspoon cayenne pepper
½ teaspoon garlic powder
2 tablespoons camelina oil
2 tablespoons semolina

MOJITO COURGETTI

This isn't an alcoholic salad, yet it tastes just like a mojito. The lovely freshness from the mint and lime is an amazing combo.

///////////// /////////////////////////////

Serves 2

1 Top and tail the courgette with a knife and then run it through your spiralizer. Chop the spiralized courgette a small bit as the strips can be very long.

2 Place the courgette into a bowl. Chop up the mint leaves and add them to the courgette along with the zest and juice of the lime, then mix. Drizzle over a small glug of olive oil and serve right away. If you want you can have the courgette spiralized in advance and dress it just before serving. It will last a day in your fridge covered with cling film. I normally serve this with a curry, but it is also incredible on its own.

1 large courgette
2 sprigs of mint
1 lime
olive oil

STUFFED SWEET POTATO SKINS

A really cheap meal to make when you are on a budget, but also an incredible side for the burrito or Cajun chicken melt. If you don't like sweet potato you can substitute some ordinary potatoes.

/////////////// ///////////////////////////////

Serves 4

1 Preheat the oven to 200ºC/400ºF/gas mark 6.

2 Pierce each sweet potato a few times with a fork all over, place on a baking tray, drizzle with the olive oil and bake for 45 minutes or until soft the whole way through.

3 Let the potatoes cool slightly, then cut in half lengthwise. Scoop out the potato flesh leaving a thin layer of sweet potato inside, and add the flesh to a large bowl. Place the skins back into the oven for 10 minutes to dry up and crisp.

4 Mash the sweet potato flesh with the milk, Parmesan and salt and pepper to taste until smooth and creamy. Remove the skins from the oven, fill each with an equal amount of potato mixture and top with the cheddar cheese. Return to the oven and bake for 15 minutes, until the cheese is melted.

5 While the potatoes are back in the oven, cook the bacon lardons. On a dry pan over a high heat, allow the lardons to go golden and crisp. Remove from the pan and drain on some kitchen paper.

6 Remove the skins from oven and top with the lardons. Serve with dollops of crème fraîche and a sprinkle of chives.

4 sweet potatoes
4 tablespoons olive oil
200ml milk
200g Parmesan, grated
sea salt and cracked black pepper to taste
200g cheddar, grated
400g bacon lardons
3 tablespoons crème fraîche
a handful of chives, chopped

STUFFING

I have used this stuffing recipe almost unaltered since the very first day I was shown how to make it. The only change is that I used to use white breadcrumbs, but now I've grown to love wholemeal instead.

///////////////// /////////////////////////////////////

Serves 4

1   Add a glug of olive oil to a large pan over a medium heat and sauté the onion for 3–4 minutes until soft.

2   Chop the herbs and add them to the pan, along with the butter. Allow the butter to melt, then stir in the breadcrumbs.

3   Add the pine nuts, cranberries and sea salt. Remove from the heat, stir through and either serve right away or place the stuffing into the oven in a casserole dish to crisp for 8–10 minutes before serving.

olive oil
1 onion, finely diced
1 sprig of sage
2 sprigs of rosemary
200g butter
200g wholemeal
  breadcrumbs
a handful of toasted pine
  nuts
a handful of dried
  cranberries chopped
a pinch of sea salt

BOXTY FRIES

Boxty is normally associated with Leitrim, Mayo, Sligo, Donegal, Longford, Fermanagh and Cavan, but you can buy a cake of boiled boxty all across Ireland now. I believe that, because we have Drummully Boxty in Cavan, it originated here. But I'll let you decide that for yourself. Boxty fries are the ultimate side to a steak. So enjoy!

///////////////// /////////////////////////////////////

Serves 2

1   Preheat the oven to 200ºC/400ºC/gas mark 6.

2   Cut the boxty into nice-sized chips. Be gentle, as it is delicate.

3   Place the chips gently onto a tray lined with parchment paper and drizzle with a good glug of oil.

4   Bake the chips in the oven for 15–20 minutes until nice and crispy. Season with sea salt, serve, and get stuck in.

1 cake of boiled boxty
rapeseed oil
sea salt to taste

DESSERTS

HEALTHY CHOCOLATE BROWNIES

These are an amazing alternative to the ordinary brownie and really help kick cravings for sweet food. They're great for anyone wanting dairy and gluten free too! The frosting is optional but it really tops them off nicely.

/////////////// ///////////////////////////////

Serves 6

1 Soak the dates in a small bowl of warm water for 15–20 minutes to soften (drain the water well afterwards).

2 Preheat your oven to 200ºC/400ºF/gas mark 6 and lightly grease a 24cm x 24cm square baking tin with coconut oil.

3 Chop up the sweet potato nice and small, then steam for about 10 minutes, until it's nicely soft.

4 Place the steamed sweet potato into a blender with the soaked dates, cacao powder, ground almonds, walnuts, almond milk, maple syrup, vanilla extract and salt. Blend together until smooth and pour into a bowl.

5 Fold in the buckwheat flour and baking powder until the mixture reaches a thick consistency, then pour the mix into the greased baking tin and bake for 20–25 minutes, until the top is nice and crisp.

6 Remove from the oven and allow to cool in the tin.

7 To make the frosting add all the frosting ingredients to a food processor and blend until smooth.

8 Once cooled, remove the brownies from the tin and spread the frosting on top, before cutting and devouring!

15 pitted Medjool dates
coconut oil for greasing, at room temperature
600g sweet potato
85g cacao powder
80g ground almonds
50g walnuts, chopped
270ml unsweetened almond milk
2 tablespoons maple syrup
1 teaspoon vanilla extract
a pinch of sea salt
100g buckwheat flour
1 teaspoon gluten-free baking powder

FOR THE CHOCOLATE FROSTING
2 avocados, peeled and destoned
2 tablespoons cacao powder
3 tablespoons honey
2 tablespoons lemon juice

3 HEALTHY ICE CREAMS

Ice cream is scientifically proven to make you happy. These three flavour combos are so quick to make and last ages in a tub in your freezer. Once you have your fruit prepped and frozen this recipe is super easy.

////////////// //////////////////////////////

Serves 4

1 Place all the ingredients into a food processor. Blend it up until really smooth and serve scoops right away. If you find it's very loose, freeze in a casserole dish for half an hour and try scooping again.

MANGO
2 mangos, peeled, chopped and frozen
zest and juice of ½ lime
2 tablespoons honey
1 tablespoon natural yoghurt (2 if needed, depending on the size of the fruit and the ice cream consistency)

STRAWBERRY AND VANILLA
2 punnets of strawberries, hulled and frozen
seeds of ½ vanilla pod
2 tablespoons honey
1 tablespoon natural yoghurt (2 if needed, depending on the size of the fruit and the ice cream consistency)

PINEAPPLE AND PASSION FRUIT
1 pineapple, peeled, chopped and frozen
juice and seeds of 3 passion fruit
2 tablespoons honey
1 tablespoon natural yoghurt (2 if needed, depending on the size of the fruit and the ice cream consistency)

HEALTHY CHOCOLATE TRUFFLES

Truffles were always served as petits fours with tea and coffee in places I've worked in. We used to hand make and temper all our chocolates. This one is a great cheat for those late night sweet cravings. They also last for ages in the freezer.

///////////////   ///////////////////////////////////////

Serves 6

1 Soak the dates in a small bowl of warm water for 10 minutes to soften (drain the water well afterwards).

2 Line a large baking sheet with parchment paper or a silicone baking mat. Set aside.

3 Place the pitted dates, vanilla extract, cocoa powder, almonds, sunflower seeds and salt (if using) into your food processor. Blend until a moist dough-like mixture forms. This will take 1–2 minutes of blending. If the mixture is too dry and crumbly, add 1–2 more soaked dates or even a teaspoon of pure maple syrup.

4 Once the dough-like consistency is achieved, scoop out 1 tablespoon. Roll it into a smooth ball, making sure to wet your hands so they don't get messy, and place on the prepared baking sheet. Repeat with remaining mixture. Set aside.

5 Heat the chocolate in a microwave in 30 second bursts, stirring after each increment, until it is completely melted and smooth. Let the warm chocolate sit for 5 minutes to slightly cool before dipping.

6 Using a spoon or your hands, dip each ball into the chocolate until it is completely covered. When lifting it out of the chocolate, tap gently on the side of the bowl to allow excess chocolate to drip off. Place each back on the baking sheet and refrigerate for about 30 minutes, until the chocolate has set. Then, of course, eat as many as you want!

14 Medjool dates
2 teaspoons vanilla extract
20g unsweetened cocoa powder
70g whole almonds
70g sunflower seeds
a pinch of sea salt (optional)
225g good quality semi-sweet or bittersweet chocolate

CHEATS AFTER EIGHT CHEESECAKE

This is an incredibly simple recipe, but just wait until you try it. It's insanely good. I truly believe that every now and again we all deserve a treat like this.

Serves 8

1 Put the digestive biscuits into a large, strong sandwich bag or tea towel and bash with a rolling pin, or put through a blender to crush up. Melt the butter over a medium heat and then pour in the crushed biscuits and mix thoroughly.

2 Put the biscuit mix into a 9-inch springform cake tin and firm down to form a compact, even layer. Place in the fridge for half an hour.

3 On a chopping board roughly chop up the contents of one box of After Eight mints and set aside.

4 Place the soft cheese and sugar into a bowl and pour in the double cream. Whisk this mix until it starts to firm. Add in the chopped dinner mints and whisk the whole mixture again.

5 Place the second box of After Eight mints standing around the inside of the cake tin so that when you remove the outside of the cake tin you are left with a 'wall' of dinner mints that are held in place by the cheesecake topping. Pour the cream cheese mixture over the top of biscuit base and smooth out with a spatula. Refrigerate for 2 hours or overnight.

6 Take the cheesecake out of the tin and place it onto a cake stand for everyone to admire in the middle of the table. Now let the boss of the house do the cutting and watch everyone demolish this.

15 digestive biscuits
56g butter
2 boxes of After Eight dinner mints
300g soft cheese
85g icing sugar
1 pint double cream

HEALTHY FRUIT CRUMBLE

This juicy berry crumble is fantastic in the winter as it tastes exactly like summer! With a subtle hint of vanilla and plenty of cinnamon streusel topping, it's the perfect dessert for any fruit lover. Cover and store any leftovers in the refrigerator for up to four days.

////////////// //////////////////////////////////

Serves 6

1 Preheat the oven to 180ºC/350ºF/gas mark 4.

2 In a small bowl, mix together the oats, flour and cinnamon. Add in the agave syrup or honey and butter, mixing until completely incorporated.

3 In another bowl, toss together the berries, cornflour and vanilla extract until thoroughly combined.

4 Spread the berry mixture in a tin or casserole dish, and evenly sprinkle the oat crumbs on top. Bake for 35–45 minutes, or until the berry juice is bubbling and the oat mixture crunchy.

5 Allow to cool slightly (so you don't burn the roof of your mouth like I have done before!), divide into bowls and serve.

95g whole oats (gluten-free if necessary)
30g wholewheat (or brown rice) flour
1 teaspoon ground cinnamon
5 tablespoons agave syrup or honey
2 tablespoons unsalted butter, melted
700g fresh (or unsweetened frozen) mixed berries
3 tablespoons cornflour
1 teaspoon vanilla extract

... r, and ginger
... the beaten eggs.
... smooth. Finally mix in

...da.
... into the prepared tin and bake
... oven for 1¼–2 hours until the
... of the tin and the centre feels firm to touch.
Check after 1¼ hours and cover with foil or double
greaseproof paper, if necessary, to prevent the top
from becoming too brown.
7. Leave in the tin for one hour. Turn out, remove
the papers and cool on a wire tray. Store in an
airtight tin.

Hint
1 level tablespoon golden syrup equals 1oz/25g
1 level tablespoon treacle equals 1oz/25g
If you heat the spoon first, the syrup or treacle will
be easier to measure.

CHOCO...

2 level...
Blended...
Boiling...
3oz	Stork M...
	(at room t...
8oz	Icing Sugar...
1 dessertspoon...
	Whiskey or M...

DECORATION
Cherries and Angelica

All-in-One Method
1. Prepare the tins (see page 7).
2. Place all the cake ingredients in a ...
and beat all the cake ingredients in a ...
(2–3 minutes)
3. Place half the mixture in each of the pre...
tins and smooth the tops.
4. Bake in the pre-heated oven for 25–30 mi...
Test (see page 7). Turn out, remove the paper
linings and cool on a wire tray.

To make Icing
5. Place all the icing ingredients in a mixing bowl
and beat until smooth and light.

To finish Cake
6. Sandwich the cakes with half the chocolate
icing.
7. Spread the remaining icing over top and swirl
with a fork.
8. Decorate with half cherries and small pieces of
angelica, previously washed and dried to remove
sugary coating.

LEFT: Gingerbread Slab Cake

Making chocolate curls

GINGERBREAD SLAB CAKE

		BAKING TIME	1¾–2 Hrs approx
		OVEN	Pre-heat to Gas Mark 4. Elec. 350°F, 180°C
		SHELF	Middle
		SIZE OF TIN	A deep 9 inch/23 cm square cake tin

IMPERIAL			METRIC
1lb	●	Plain Flour	450g
	●	8 level teaspoons Ground Ginger	
	●	1 level teaspoon Bread Soda	
½ pint		Milk	275ml
8oz		Stork Margarine	225g
8oz		Brown Sugar	225g
6oz		Golden Syrup	175g
6oz		Treacle	175g
	●	2 Eggs (size 1 or 2) whisked lightly	

...od
... ke tins (see page 7).
...d beat together with a wooden spoon until well
mixed (2–3 minutes).
3. Divide mixture in half. To one half add the
peppermint essence and green colouring and to
the other half add the cooled chocolate mixture in the
4. Place alternate spoonfuls of the mixture in the
prepared tins and smooth the tops.
5. Bake in the pre-heated oven for 25–30 minutes.
Test (see page 7). Turn out, remove the paper
lining and cool on a wire tray.

To make Chocolate Fudge Icing
6. Place all the icing ingredients together in a bowl
over hot water. Remove from
7. Beat until the mixture is smooth. Remove from
the heat and leave until cold. Beat well until thick
enough to spread.

... Milk Flake Bar

22

Tea Brack   2lb Loaf Tins

                                       170°/300 f

12 oz   Dried mixed fruit   1 hr

8 oz   SR Flour

1 egg

2 heaped   teaspoon of mixed spice

1/2   "   "   Nutmeg

1 Mug   Cold Tea.

Sleep fruit in   Cold Tea   overnight
nutmeg & spices as well
Next day add flour

A COUPLE OF COCKTAILS

I'm a little bit cheeky putting some cocktails in here. But we are all guilty of enjoying these on occasion. There is no harm every now and again in letting your hair down, throwing on a nice shirt and drinking a cocktail.

MOJITO

Serves 1

1   Cut the lime into four wedges. Add to a glass, then add the sugar and muddle (squish everything together with a muddler, the back of a wooden spoon, or even a rolling pin) to release some of the lime juice.

2   Rub the mint leaves around the rim of the glass and drop them in. Using your muddler, gently push the mint down into the lime juice and wedges.

3   Half fill the glass with crushed ice, then pour in the Bacardi. Stir the mix together until the sugar dissolves.

4   Top up with crushed ice, a splash of the soda water and garnish with a sprig of mint and wedge of lime.

½ fresh lime, well washed
1 heaped tablespoon caster sugar
8 fresh mint leaves
2 handfuls of ice cubes, crushed
a good glug of Bacardi (I'll let you measure)
a dash of soda water to fill the glass
a sprig of fresh mint and a wedge of lime to garnish

STRAWBERRY DAIQUIRI

Lads, if you're having a Daiquiri, order it in a pint glass so you still look manly!

/////////////// ///////////////////////////////

Serves 2

1 Place the strawberries, sugar, rum, vanilla seeds, lime juice and ice cubes into a blender or Nutribullet and whizz until smooth. Serve in glasses and garnish with the mint.

1 pack fresh strawberries (green trimmed off)
2 tablespoons sugar or honey
60ml rum
seeds of ½ vanilla pod
juice of 1 lime
a handful of ice cubes
2 sprigs of fresh mint to garnish

INDEX

I'd like to dedicate this book to my Granny Annie Sheridan, an amazing cook. Her Hasselback potato recipe, which I loved as a kid, is included. I'm sure she's looking down, still calling me Donald Duck and Biscuit Face!

MERCIER PRESS

Cork

www.mercierpress.ie

© Adrian Martin, 2017

www.chefadrian.ie

Photographed by Rob Kerkvliet –
www.afoxinthekitchen.com

Styled by Zita Fox –
www.afoxinthekitchen.com

ISBN: 978 1 78117 490 6

10 9 8 7 6 5 4 3 2 1

A CIP record for this title is available from the British Library

Printed and bound in the EU.